*Through the*

**Finalist for the 2021 City of Victoria Butler Book Prize**

"This book is a glimpse into forty years of intimacy—what it means to adore, endure, defy, devote, grieve. It is a witnessing of final days—ardent with longing, aching candour, and a powerful tenderness."
—Anne Michaels, author of *Fugitive Pieces*

"Emotionally brave and profoundly tender, this book will introduce you to beautifully wrought gardens of poetry, and to two deeply creative individuals who, side by side, flourished in those gardens. A moving and life-affirming reading experience."
—Jane Urquhart, author of *The Stone Carvers*

"Lorna Crozier gives us the flesh-and-blood thrill of becoming a poet, and then the high romance of finding and losing the poet she loves. Her passionate memoir is unabashed and never less than fascinating."
—Elizabeth Hay, author of *All Things Consoled*

"With feet bare and a heart full of love and longing, Lorna Crozier walks us back to the beginnings of our own fragile bones and back to the place where roots hold us until we become them, until we are the love we planted." —Gregory Scofield, author of *Witness, I Am*

"To read Lorna Crozier's memoir is to follow two legends of Canadian letters down an enchanted garden path, through the early days of their boozy, Carver-esque romance to the final destination of an endless, timeless love. Overflowing with poetry, wisdom, and cats, this book demands re-reading, for your heart may struggle to hold it all."
—Marjorie Celona, author of *How a Woman Becomes a Lake*

"A work of searing intensity, *Through the Garden* stands as a testament to poetry, love, and longing. Chronicling her fiery romance with her husband, the poet Patrick Lane, and his subsequent descent into a mysterious illness, Lorna Crozier reminds us that remembering lies at the heart of who we are. This is one of the great love stories of our time."

—Steven Price, author of *Lampedusa*

"In *Through the Garden,* Lorna Crozier lays a path between life's two great mysteries—love and death. Her gaze is honest and steady, never faltering, whether examining her own heart or looking into the eyes of her dying partner. Out of such bold courage comes a book that is like love—agonizing and joyful, replete with poetry and story, a wellspring of wisdom and truth."

—Merilyn Simonds, author of *Refuge*

"Lorna Crozier's *Through the Garden* draws us into a rich and intimate portrait of the tender, turbulent lives of two writers who shared a love affair with words, cats, the world, and each other for some forty years. As Crozier's husband, writer Patrick Lane, is overtaken by illness and she by grief, this book reminds us that memory, like history, makes us who we are and outruns death. Elegantly written and searingly frank, *Through the Garden* drills deep into the personal while ranging outward to confront the storms and mysteries of life."

—2020 Hilary Weston Writers' Trust Prize for Nonfiction jury (Helen Knott, Sandra Martin, and Ronald Wright)

"Attuned to seasonal rhythms and just as moving. There are moments of joy and lyrical description, and stretches of unflinching honesty."

—*Maclean's*

# Through the Garden

A Love Story (with Cats)

# Through the Garden

## A Love Story (with Cats)

### Lorna Crozier

McClelland & Stewart

Pages 67, 177–8: Reprinted with permission from *Beauty by Design* by Bill Terry and
Rosemary Bates, 2013 TouchWood Editions. Copyright © 2013 by Bill Terry. Page 85:
Lines from "Thoreau Said a Walk Changes the Walker" Extract rights from *The Wild in
You: Voices from the Forest and the Sea* by Lorna Crozier, photographs by Ian McAllister,
published by Greystone Books Ltd. Page 139: "Breakage" and page 207: "A Small Ambition"
were first published in *The House the Spirit Builds*, photographs by Peter Coffman and
Diane Laundy (Douglas & McIntyre, 2019). Page 178: "Tell the Ones You Love" from
*Heart Residence: Collected Poems 1967–2017* copyright © 2017 by Dennis Lee. Reproduced
with permission from House of Anansi Press, Toronto. www.houseofanansi.com. Page 193:
"Self-Centred" was first published in *What the Soul Doesn't Want* (Freehand Books, 2017).

All excerpts from *There Is a Season* and *Deep River Night* by Patrick Lane © Patrick Lane
and reprinted by permission of McClelland & Stewart.

Pages 25 and 76: excerpts from "Close" and "Bokuseki" by Patrick Lane, *Washita* (Harbour
Publishing, 2014). Page 135: excerpt from "Wisteria" by Patrick Lane, *Selected Poems:
1977–1997* (Harbour Publishing, 1997). Page 164: excerpts from "The Bird" and "The
Man" by Patrick Lane, *The Collected Poems of Patrick Lane* (Harbour Publishing, 2011).
www.harbourpublishing.com.

All excerpts from poems by Lorna Crozier © Lorna Crozier and reprinted by permission
of McClelland & Stewart.

Library and Archives Canada Cataloguing in Publication
Title: Through the garden : a love story (with cats) / Lorna Crozier.
Names: Crozier, Lorna, 1948- author.
Identifiers: Canadiana 20200191608 | ISBN 9780771021244 (softcover)
Subjects: LCSH: Crozier, Lorna, 1948-—Marriage. | LCSH: Lane, Patrick—Marriage. |
CSH: Poets, Canadian (English)—Biography. | CSH: Authors, Canadian (English)—
Biography. | LCSH: Authors' spouses—Canada—Biography. | LCGFT: Autobiographies.
Classification: LCC PS8555.R72 Z46 2021 | DDC C811/.54—dc23

Cover design: Emma Dolan
Cover images: (photograph) Bob Siemens; (photo frame) Krasovski Dmitri / Shutterstock;
(Cherry blossoms) xiangyan meng/Getty Images; (Paper sheet) Flavio Coelho/
Getty Images; (rope) NYS444/iStock/Getty Images

Photo page 213: Rafal Gerszak

Printed in Canada

McClelland & Stewart,
a division of Penguin Random House Canada Limited,
a Penguin Random House Company

www.penguinrandomhouse.ca

1 2 3 4 5     25 24 23 22 21

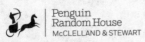
Penguin
Random House
McCLELLAND & STEWART

For my beloved, Patrick Lane, who wrote,
"your hand in my hand in the dark."

# Through the Garden

## A Love Story (with Cats)

POEM ME

I came to him that first night and said, Poem me.
And he did.
He came to me that first night and said, Poem me.
And I did.
Of our hours we made a poem.
Of our years we made a poem.
Many things happened in between.
Many things were rubbed out, repeated,
neglected, ignored, stained, thrown away.
But this morning he said, Poem me.
This morning I said, Poem me.
And we made of our lives a poem.

*This morning I am full of prayer though I do not utter it. I pray all goes well this fine morning. Lorna is back from her retreat. I've just seen her at the kitchen door in her red robe. She is letting the cats out and once they're on the deck she calls my name as if it were a question and I answer and say, I'm here, here in the garden. She comes to me then with two cups of coffee and as she walks across the moss I see what beauty is and am undone by it. I say to her, You are beautiful, and she smiles as she comes to me barefoot, her feet wet with dew.*

*Pray God, there may be many more days, I whisper.*

Patrick Lane, *There Is a Season*

## February, 2017

SPRING COMES EARLY to Vancouver Island. It's still a surprise though it's been twenty-seven years since we moved to the rain coast. There are many advantages to this temperate climate, some not as obvious as the early return of the male robins or the snow-drops whitening the borders of our front lawn instead of real snow. If we have to euthanize our cat and bury him, the ground will not be frozen eight feet down, as it is until late April in Saskatchewan, where I was born. We'll dig, and the winter earth will give. It will open up to take his tawny, long-haired, skinny, beloved body.

This is some comfort, I guess.

"The naming of cats is a difficult matter," claimed T.S. Eliot. For all of his brilliance and his affection for his feline companions, perhaps he didn't know that cats love to carry the names of poets into the world. Eighteen years ago when we chose from the litter this male who looked like a small, blue-eyed cloud, we named him Basho, after the Japanese haiku master. Like his namesake, our Basho practices *karumi*, a lightness on his paws and a lightness in his spirit that lets him greet the world as it is whether he's feeling well or out of sorts, whether he's decided to walk alone or in our company. The choice is his. This morning he's chosen to doze close to where I am weeding, curled like a worn, tossed-away rug on the newly stirring earth, letting the day go on with its business as he dreams what cats dream when they are old.

Baudelaire said that you can tell the time by looking in the eyes of a cat. Basho's time is running out. He's been diagnosed with kidney failure; we have to give him intravenous water and vitamin shots twice a week. I also rub an ointment on the inside of his ear to titillate his appetite. Even so, I stalk him in the house several times a day with a bowl full of food I hope will spark his hunger. Too often he turns his head away with elegant disdain. Thinking about the world without him makes me panic—my breath catches in my chest like a broken flying thing.

Trowel in hand, I pause to look at him, to memorize the two skinny strokes of charcoal smudged from the outer corner of each eye to the top of his mocha-coloured head, to note again the exact place where his ear is notched, the fringes of his long coat, the length and texture of the thick tufts between his toes as if he was born to walk on snow, the bump of a scar on his dark nose from a long-ago spat. I could sit with him here for hours as he curls in sleep, basking in the calmness that he breathes into the world, but the garden doesn't slow down, doesn't wait for me to catch up. It's not only snowdrops that are flourishing. The back end of our property, around two-thirds of an acre on the north end of the Saanich peninsula on this far-western island, has sprung alive with unwanted green and if I want to stop its spreading, I have to get at it. That's okay. Pulling out the first blurts of February fecundity is one of the few things I have control of. It is good, physical labour whose results are immediately obvious to even an amateur gardener's eye.

## IN MOONLIGHT

Something moves
just beyond the mind's
clumsy fingers.

It has to do with seeds.
The earth's insomnia.
The garden going on
without us

needing no one to watch it
not even the moon.

The weed that claims the beginning of the season as its own is a ground-hugging, small-leaved splat the size of a tea saucer called hairy bittercress; its Latin, *Cardimine hirsuta*. My name for it is simpler and monosyllabic—*pest*. In the dampness of early morning, I patrol the beds, yank it with little effort from the mud, shake its roots, and drop it into a bucket. Under the tap I rinsed my plunder last spring and tore it up for salad, thinking I'd find it as tasty as foraging gourmands find dandelions, but the peppery-flavoured leaves were too minuscule and difficult to clean, not to mention the hairy part of the hirsuta's roots. Now I toss a bounty of them in the back of the pickup. I'll wait for a full load of garden stuff and then drive to the compost place and get rid of it so the atoms can be converted into a beneficial, unweedy substance that will jump-start the soil next spring. The garden is a good place in this season of woe and worry to remember that energy transmutes into energy: nothing disappears.

Patrick, the man I've been living with for almost forty years, is in the garden too. It's a treat to have him home: he spent the last three weeks in the hospital with a high fever, chills, and sweats. It was an emergency admittance. His doctor, one of the internal-medicine hotshots in the Acute Care Clinic at the Victoria General Hospital, took one look at him and said, "You're staying here."

Several months before Patrick's first hospital stay, pain began an assault on his body, occupying one zone then moving relentlessly to another. One morning his neck and shoulders stiffened and his upper body froze. We attributed this rigidity to the hours he'd spent hunched over the computer working on his new novel. He was in no shape to teach, but a year ago he'd signed up to lead a three-day workshop at a retreat centre about two hours away. I had to pull some stuff together, rush off, and fill in; many of those registered had flown from other provinces to work with him, and he couldn't just cancel.

By the time I got back home, the rigor had disappeared, but he felt as if a metal wire was being yanked tight around his forehead, the ache so unbearable our family doctor thought he had a brain bleed and sent him for a scan. Then his right leg ballooned and reddened from knee to ankle, and I couldn't touch him anywhere—his skin was too tender. He lost his appetite, he was breathless, he couldn't sleep. Not his heart but the bones that caged his heart smarted when he woke up. There were nights he spiked a fever and his side of the bed was soaked by morning. The markers in his blood that indicated a serious infection regularly went off the chart.

He was released from the hospital after three weeks of intravenous antibiotics and tests, including a search for a cardiac infection. Not one of the seven specialists who pinched and prodded and asked long lists of questions proffered a diagnosis. What he has is some kind of autoimmune disorder, but the big names they've thrown at him—giant cell arteritis, polymyalgia rheumatica, vasculitis—don't stick. His symptoms jump the borders of the doctors' expertise. Once they ruled out problems with his heart, they tested for tumours, for Lyme disease, for bone marrow cancer, for tropical infections he might have picked up years ago in South America, and finally for strange syndromes we'd never heard of, including something called "Whipple disease." When the technician took vials of blood for this rare condition, she asked, "Have you been in any Nordic countries? Have you been around sheep?"

This man who has never complained about the state of his health keeps saying that something isn't right, that he feels sick deep inside. "You're a mystery, Mr. Lane," his practitioners say, one by one. It's the last thing a patient wants to hear. They load him up with antibiotics, painkillers, and Prednisone, a high-powered steroid that doesn't get rid of the underlying cause but props him up with a cardboard crutch until a diagnosis and treatment can be found. *If* they can be found. All we know for sure is that he is ill, and his illness is devastating to us both.

Patrick steps down off the deck to trim the plumes of yellow and red grasses he planted last fall along the shores of a dry stream we laid, stone by stone, outside his office window after we cut down two huge laurels that blocked his view. (It wasn't as though we had a shortage of laurels. There are more than a dozen throughout the yard, all of them requiring pruning every year.) I try not to watch him. He works only ten minutes or so before he stops, stands upright, and musters the strength to boost himself onto the deck again. It rises only a foot above the ground, but he strains to lift his legs, one and then the other, as if they've morphed into tree stumps. It's hard for him to keep his balance. A fall could be catastrophic. The unforgiving drugs have eaten away at his bones and if they break, they may not mend.

Last July, sitting inside at my desk on the other side of a sliding glass door that faces the back yard, I watched three baby raccoons attempt the same task as Patrick. They'd been hiding—not nesting, I'd hoped—in the darkness under the deck. They tried to heave themselves from the stone stream, first by placing their front paws on the edge of the planks, then struggling to hoist their chubby haunches. The biggest of the three did it with no trouble, swinging up his left back leg, then his right. His siblings had as much difficulty as Patrick—more, really, because they *did* fall, tumbling backwards, then righting themselves and trying again. I could hear the mother chittering encouragement, though I couldn't see her. After three tries the second kit hauled himself up and scuffled towards her in that hunch-backed perambulatory style particular to their kind. Because of the oxymoronic way raccoons move—lumbering and graceful, galumphing and lissome—you'd guess they shared ancestors with both the bear and the weasel. Patrick described them perfectly: a ballerina with a wrestler's shoulders.

The runt looked like it wasn't going to make it. What if I interfered and gave it a boost with my foot? The nature of these animals made me pause. Their sweet-looking faces belie their fierceness. Their claws are serious weapons: throw a raccoon into an action movie and it would win against any kenjutsu. Their deft fingers are usually employed in more peaceful though annoying-to-a-gardener tasks, like plucking water hyacinths from the pond or flipping over the moss and our carefully arranged stones to look for grubs. "Raccoon" comes to English from the Algonquin word *arakum*; its translation—"he who scratches with his hand"—highlights the nimbleness of the animal's forepaws. It's easy to imagine him doing more creative things with his long, spreadable fingers.

GAME

By the pond at night
three raccoons play
paper, scissors, rock.
They have the hands
to do it. When they get bored
they turn ahead the clocks
while you lie sleeping.
That's why, no matter
what your age, by dawn
your time is up.

Maybe it was the mother's increasingly loud chatter that gave the littlest one a shot of dexterity and oomph. After a few more clumsy attempts, it clambered up and scuttled in the direction of her calls. I stepped outside to see where the family had gone. Near the kitchen door I heard a low growl halfway up the pollarded pine tree. The mother stared down at me through her black outlaw mask, her babies safely tucked behind her in the deeper shadows of the branches.

One night when we were watching TV, through the high window above the screen we glimpsed an adult raccoon climb to the top of the gate post then leap the foot and a half onto the roof, his golden under-belly for a moment exposed. Another big guy followed, then another. Three brawny parkour artists ascending to the full moon that hung low in the sky. Like my childhood buddies and I planning to rendezvous at a favourite spot, had this gang of friends arranged to gather at the peak of our roof to sit side by side, staring at the sky? "Let's meet on the roof to watch the moon." Perhaps in another mother tongue this masked, dextrous mammal is known as "He who cups the moon in his hands."

There's a second cat in the garden with us this morning, a crazy four-year-old tortoiseshell stretching her paws above her head to shred one of the cedar stumps that holds Patrick's bonsai. "Bonsai" isn't exactly the right word: Patrick can't bear to hurt the seedlings that he finds growing around the Japanese maple in our yard and transplants into shallow pots. Instead of twisting them and using wire to force them into contorted shapes, he simply trims judiciously, his astute, aesthetic eye creating a pleasing, untortured miniature that resembles the real thing. Though stunted, the little trees seem happy.

For our tortoiseshell's name, once again we looked to a poet, this time the ninth-century Chinese sage Po Chu-I. Since she's female, we should address her as *Lady* Po Chu-I, but in the way of humans who don't know any better and who love diminutives, we call her Po. Basho hates her, partly because she zooms in like a furry, four-legged shark to raid his bowl if he looks away. Even if he turns his nose up at his food, her forays must seem an insult to his dignity and his seigniorial rights in the kingdom of our household.

After Patrick's release from the hospital this month I've asked him nearly every morning, "Are you feeling better today?" His body's baffling attack on itself saps his vitality. He gets out of bed, does something as undemanding as eat breakfast, and lies down again. He tells me it takes every ounce of gumption he has to swing his legs onto the floor. The other day, he tried to carry our three emptied recycling boxes from the end of the long driveway to the house. He managed only one and had to flip it upside down and sit on it, catching his breath until he could continue. One stop and then another and then another. For weeks, I've sounded like a beggar, my words a plea that everything will be okay, that we'll get back to normal. I overheard him tell a friend on the phone that worse than being sick and hospitalized is watching me fret and hearing my desperate implorations that he'll wake up well.

I could query, "How are you this morning?" That's a less demanding, less hope-laden question than "Are you feeling better?" Or, better yet, I could simply say "good morning" and not ask anything at all. Basho, also worryingly ill, is less irritated with me than Patrick. Because he doesn't understand much of my language—perhaps he chooses not to—I don't annoy him, except to follow him around with food as Po Chu lurks around a corner, hoping I won't notice her and so forget to pick up his bowl. There's a condition called "starving-cat syndrome." She's got it. She was a famished eight-month-old cat when she was found abandoned, and her fear of hunger devours her. Her stomach never registers as "full."

From THOMAS HARDY'S HEART

I am the cat who swallowed
Thomas Hardy's heart. I snatched it
from the bowl in my mistress's kitchen
and leapt through the window to the woods.

She was his sister.
What was she going to do with it?
Stuff it with veal and breadcrumbs?
Soak it in cider and serve it with the funeral meats?

It pumped a trail across the sill
and then the paving stones,
pounding out its life. I believe
she'll never get over it,

such screams and shrieking, her face
drunk with tears.

Plump as a rat and slippery,
he would have said *the deadest thing*
—it was the strangest thing
I've ever eaten. In the mouth it was sweet;
in the belly, all wormwood and rue.

Better than a tongue, a bitter heart
speaks truly. I had nine lives.
Now I've ten . . .

Po Chu wouldn't be a part of our family if it weren't for Patrick.
When we brought her home, courtesy of the same animal-rescue
group that had introduced us to Basho as a kitten fourteen years
before, I was leery of her. Basho was too. She was found thin and
dehydrated, alone and howling, trapped on a concrete median
between two streams of traffic in an industrial part of the city,
but like the poet Po Chu-I, who outlasted nine emperors, she
survived.

Though she appeared to be no more than a fleshless pelt draped
over the bones of a cat, we knew she'd had kittens because the teats
on the sagging skin of her belly were fat with milk. Perhaps the
loss of her litter forged a link with her namesake: his most famous
poem is a long narrative called "Song of Everlasting Sorrow."
There was a mournful undertone, her rescuers claimed, to her
cries. She's never learned to meow—the sound she makes to get
attention is a cross between a whimper and a squeak. I've never
come across anything from a cat that slips with such a sting into
the heart. I like to think she knew Po Chu-I's mournful song.

How could anyone who cares for cats resist her ancient and contemporary lament?

By the time we met her, she'd gained a pound, which is a lot for a small animal, but her coat remained thin and dry, and a hairy spike stuck up on the top of her head as if stiffened with Kool-Aid gel. She could have been cousin to one of those strange Polish chickens with an orange feathered crown—the kind that constantly bob their heads and look deranged. Po Chu's yellow eyes, equally as mad, sparked when she looked at us. They could have lit dry tinder.

We crated her to our house and isolated her in the guest bedroom with a screen over the doorway until she and Basho could adapt to each other's presence. He growled every time he stopped to sniff. He'd been the *numero uno* four-legged animal in our house and I didn't want his status to change any more than he did. In human terms he was in his nineties; surely he deserved to be dominant or, at least, respected. When I'd go in to feed Po Chu and change the litter box, I'd try to touch her. She'd spit at me and leap out of reach. "Be patient," Patrick said. "She'll get used to us."

As soon as we took the screen off, she chased Basho into the library—the last room down our rancher's long hall—and he wouldn't come out. I didn't want the end of his life to be so constricted and stressful. For weeks I didn't know what to do. I called to him from the kitchen and the living room and rattled his bag of treats, which normally he'd come running for, but he wouldn't budge. One morning, a couple of months after her arrival, he'd had enough. I watched him meet her in the middle of the hall. Whereas before he'd slink against the wall and backtrack, this time he glared head-on and batted her with a big forepaw. She jumped as if struck with a taser. And that was all it took. He became the boss again and wandered the house at will. Less mobile four years later, mostly blind and deaf, now he just has to stare at her—no matter what he can see—and she steals away, sometimes under the bed till he wobbles past. In the way of cats, they worked it out, but they'll never like each other. I wonder what we humans can learn from that.

Basho's victory didn't solve Po's relationship with us. If we came too close, she'd hiss, hair electric, then slash our arms or legs. I read online that you should move toward a cat when it claws or bites, not away, or it will assume you're prey and quicken its attack. If you do the opposite, the cat will retreat. Not Po Chu. When her claws dug in and I stretched my arm toward her instead of jerking it back, she didn't let go but raked her way up from my wrist to my forearm to my bicep. No wonder I avoided touching her or picking her up.

Never mind the lack of companionship and the absence of any comfort or cuddling from this cat—how were we going to take her to the vet for her inoculations? How could we comb her long hair so it wouldn't get matted or clip her nails or check her for fleas or ticks or injuries? The rescue agency had told us we could return her if she didn't fit into our family. Still afraid to go near her, I called the woman in charge. "No," she asserted, "you can't bring her back. We have no room for her. You'll have to drop her off at the SPCA."

The SPCA? No one would take her home. She'd live in a cage forever.

Patrick hadn't wanted me to make the phone call in the first place. He said, "She's just scared. I'll work on her. You stay out of it." We could tell she'd been abused. If you lowered your hand toward her, she flinched. If you gently tried to nudge her with your foot when she paused in the open doorway as most cats do, she'd cringe and then lash out. Someone had kicked her, punched her, perhaps thrown her across the room. That someone had tossed her away when she became pregnant or after she'd borne her litter. It's likely that same someone had also done away with her kittens.

For a month I watched Patrick pick her up by finding her blind spot and scooping her from behind before she knew what he was doing. Then he'd hold her with his arms crossed and press down to lock her paws so she couldn't strike. She was so shocked she didn't bite, and anyway, she couldn't turn her head around for her jaws to reach and her teeth to sink in. "You are such a good girl, Po Chu," he chanted in a soft voice, "such a good girl. We love you." He'd also pluck her from the couch when she was sleeping and wedge her into the narrow space between his hip and the arm of the easy chair. The weight of his forearm across her back trapped her legs beneath her and held her still. Every muscle, every sinew tensed. "Oh, Po Chu, you are so sweet! Such a good cat. We love you."

She did not want to be there; she did not want to be lifted or held or touched, but day after day he picked her up, ran his fingers across her cheeks where cats like to be stroked and scratched the top of her head and under her collar. Gradually, she stopped struggling in the easy chair beside him. Along his thigh where it pressed against her, he could feel the engine of her body start up as if he'd pulled a rope on a furry, miniature motor. She was purring. One evening when he was reading, she jumped up beside him and snuggled into her old spot. Quietly, so as not to disturb her, he called me from the kitchen to see. She raised her chin to be scratched.


Ours has been a public love story, Patrick's and mine, shared in poems and books and in interviews on CBC. In the national press, we've been called "one of Canada's powerhouse literary couples," and we've talked openly about what it's like for two writers to live together. My written words are inextricably linked to his. Our offices, converted from bedrooms in the house where we've lived since 2006, sit side by side. I can roll back my chair, lean out my study door and see his back as he sits at his computer. Frequently, one of us will raise their voice, only slightly, and ask, "How do you spell . . . ?" Before we send anything out or give a talk, we ask the other to edit what we've done, and each of us is merciless, our pens slashing across the page.

Because we respect each other, when it's necessary we dare to say, "This isn't good enough—you have to start over." We're critical even of the poems we dedicate "For Patrick," or "For Lorna." When he passes me a piece of paper with words I know are meant for me, I ask, "Do you want me to just enjoy this or edit it?" "Enjoy," he says. And I do. I do. And he does too. I can't help but think that a passage from Virginia Woolf's *Mrs. Dalloway* could have had us in mind: "He thought her beautiful, believed her impeccably wise; dreamed of her, wrote poems to her, which, ignoring the subject, she corrected in red ink."

When we ran off together in 1978, abandoning our marriages and leaving wreckage in our wake, I was a "promising writer"; Patrick had just won the Governor General's Award. I was so happy for him, and I've continued to be every time an honour comes his way, but I knew if I didn't grow, if I remained merely someone who showed potential, we wouldn't last. I swore I wouldn't play the dutiful wife, cheerleader, and muse of the great male writer, and he didn't envision a partner like that. I didn't want to grow pale and bitter in his shadow or be worn thin by professional jealousy. We aspired to flourish together and thrive in words and books and gardens.

Mary Pratt, whose pictures and interviews I turn to for inspiration and guidance, has fearlessly documented the difficulties of living with a revered male artist who works in the same field.

When Christopher Pratt's reputation shone brighter than hers near the beginning of their careers, she sought counsel from one of her former university teachers and mentors, Lawren Harris, the son of the Group of Seven luminary he was named after. Harris told her there was room for only one painter per household, and at the Pratts', that wasn't her. I can't help but think of the courage and self-confidence she had to rally to ignore that advice from someone who'd praised her early work. Though she was born thirteen years before me, the world hadn't changed that much by the time Patrick and I moved in together. I needed to find the same belief in myself that she was able to muster and hold on to it, no matter what accolades or harsh counsel came his or my way.

I've never met Mary Pratt, but several times I sat across a restaurant table or shared a literary stage with one of my other role models, the novelist Carol Shields. Coincidentally, both she and Pratt were born the same year, 1935. From the time Carol and I met, I admired her dedication to her craft, her generosity with younger writers, and her refusal of the easy gesture or phrase. If you were lucky enough to meet her for lunch or a glass of wine, she wouldn't allow an escape into small talk. Within a few minutes—longer, perhaps, if you'd started by talking about shoes—you'd be involved in an in-depth discussion about things that mattered.

Toward the end of Carol's life, she and her husband settled in a character home in Victoria, about a half hour drive from Patrick and me. After she'd gone through a round of chemotherapy for breast cancer, she delivered her honorary doctorate address for the University of Winnipeg in her gracious living room because she was too ill to travel. It was 1996, and Carol's two main pieces of advice were aimed at the young women who would have made up the majority of liberal arts graduates at the Manitoba convocation. "Choose your partner wisely," she said to the small group of family members, dignitaries, and friends who had gathered. "And always act as smart as you are." That last bit struck home. During my adolescence in small-town Saskatchewan, girls of my generation were told to dumb ourselves down and let boys win in any competition. If you beat them, you'd never get a date; you'd be the one sitting home alone on Saturday night waiting for the phone to ring.

For years I'd mocked that sexist message—it even became a joke among me and my women friends—but going by my visceral reaction to Carol's words, I realized I hadn't completely erased it from my brain. Or was it the word *always* that got me? "*Always* act as smart as you are." Was I still, in subtle ways and on occasion, being less than what I could be so I wouldn't lose the man whom I wanted to adore me? Was it easier for me to celebrate my brilliant companion's successes than to appreciate my own? I don't think he'd have asked the same questions about himself—at least, I'd never sensed that.

When I heard that I'd been made an Officer of the Order of Canada, two years before Patrick received the same recognition, my delight lasted merely seconds before I burst into tears on the phone with the francophone official from the Governor General's office in Ottawa. "This should have been Patrick's," I blubbered.

She paused, then said, "Be that as it may, this time it is you." I dreaded telling him the news. When I did, he said, "How great is that?" but a strained expression flickered across his face and tempered his words with an unspoken "Why not me?"

We never talked about it, but I understood why he might respond that way. He was the older writer, one of the country's most celebrated and respected poets, with more publications under his belt than I could claim. And his memoir, *There Is a Season*, was nothing short of brilliant. Alice Munro, who rarely tendered book blurbs, wrote for the cover, "To read this book is to enter a state of enchantment." There's no question that he deserved the honour, but was it necessary for me to feel that I didn't? In saying, "This should have been yours," what stupid lesson from my childhood was I enacting? Why didn't I have more faith in him, and why did I feel the need to dampen my own pleasure until I almost washed it away? He didn't ask me to do that, and his reaction, as far as I could tell, was short-lived.

Mary Pratt, on the other hand, in a sad revelation after she and Christopher parted, disclosed a darker side of her famous husband. "He got jealous whenever anything happened for me. I guess I shouldn't be surprised by that, but I was. He and I had always developed together." It was a woman's dilemma she was talking about: if her career hadn't soared, if she'd remained the secondary figure, the housewife and mother, merely a dabbler in art, their marriage might have lasted.

In our years together, there's been the odd flicker of jealousy from each of us, but we've survived our sometimes less-than-admirable feelings (yes, we are only human, I say to myself) because we don't let them hang around for long. Like grains of dust, envy, competitiveness, and self-pity blow through the screen door of the back porch, where we get at them with a broom and sweep them out before they can sift into the inner rooms that provide a haven for our hours in each other's company. Our unwavering support of one another's decision to live our lives as poets, however risky and fraught, and our genuine pleasure in each other's success—these characterize, above all else, the forty years we've spent side by side dreaming our words into the world. It is a strange obsession to have, this passion for poetry, and surely it demands a pledge to love and support the one who balances beside you on a line of words stretched thin as hope over an abyss of self-doubt and fear and probable obscurity.

———

Winnipeg was our first city. We started off there when Patrick took up the position of writer-in-residence at the University of Manitoba in the fall of 1978. I had a Canada Council grant, my first, and was working on a new poetry manuscript. We wrote and fought and drank and made love—everything with such burning intensity, people who knew us thought we wouldn't make it through the year. We didn't think so either.

One night we shouted at each other in the kitchen of our rented suite in the city's north end as six guests sat around the table in the dining room waiting for us to serve dinner. "I've had enough," I told him and ran into the bedroom to throw some things into a bag. Patrick said, "You're not leaving, *I* am," and we pushed past each other out the front door like unruly children, me jumping in the car and he in his truck, leaving our guests behind, the roast he'd been carving bleeding on the cutting board, the spuds half-mashed in the pot, the potato masher stuck in the middle, milk slopped on the counter. At least we'd turned off the stove. One of the women around the table told me weeks later that nobody knew what to do. "Are they coming back? Should we wait?"

I drove around the block and pulled over to the curb, feeling stupid, not knowing where to go. After about an hour I retraced my route, parked on our street, and walked to the house. All the lights were on, the table set, the food as we'd left it in the kitchen, and no one was there. Patrick arrived a few minutes later. We started laughing, poured ourselves the dregs of the wine, and soon tumbled into bed. Other nights, both of us drinking heavily, Patrick lobbed a tumbler against the wall to punctuate his frustration at something I'd said. I annoyed him so much the evening before he was to leave for a two-week reading tour of the Atlantic provinces that he stared coldly at me, then smashed his glasses with a flat stone we used as a coaster. It was an I'll-show-you gesture. He was blind without his glasses, and there was no time to replace them. I didn't know how he was going to make the trip.

A few days into it, I fielded a call from a Dalhousie professor, who asked where Patrick was. He hadn't shown up for his reading in Nova Scotia. I found out later that Patrick hadn't made it out of Newfoundland, the first stop on his tour, not because he couldn't see where he was going but because he'd partied with a gang of poets and musicians in St. John's the night before his departing flight and missed his morning plane to Halifax.

After one of our fiercest arguments—I can't remember now what it was about—I ran to my desk, wrote a poem and hurled it at him like an Irish wisp:

I pour your coffee
down the drain
Violence, you push me
to violence, you say
Why do you want
the animal in me?

I burn your poems
scatter the ashes over your toast
wait for you to split me
in two like the flat fish
fashioned into sky

Instead you must talk
explain my perversions
ask: What do you want?

Patrick read my poem then banged out a response on his manual typewriter. He used just two fingers to type, one to peck the keys like a chicken on speed and another to hit the return carriage. I could hear the bang and clatter.

The space
between my ribs contains
only a loss. As a child
I dreamed the story of the
mother made from me
and lying alone in bed
counted my cage of bone
the stolen life.

In that turning wheel
called darkness
where dreams, impossible
as fish, swim below
the hunched carapace
that is the sky,
I swim, endlessly
imagining my escape.

"Huh," I said, "imagining your escape, indeed!" I wrote another poem and he responded. When the anger wore off, we became interested in the linguistic spat not as an explosion of emotions but as a dialogue between two writers. Over the next several weeks, we created a series of poems that talked, side-stepped, retreated and collided with one another. A male and female voice sparring and dancing and catching breath in the silence that settled for a moment in between. It became a challenge to hone the call and response, to turn our tinder, our furor, into art. Four months after the exchange began, we published a fifty-one-page collection called *No Longer Two People* with Turnstone Press in Winnipeg.

It was the wrong title. We chose it to protect ourselves, to give us some distance from the personal nature of the writing and to claim that though the poems started in the real world they were a fiction, an invention, an abstraction of our actual lives. The title comes from a quotation by Pablo Picasso and we used it as an epigraph: "Though these two people once existed for me, they exist no longer. The 'vision' of them gave me a preliminary emotion; then little by little their actual presences became blurred; they developed into a fiction and then disappeared altogether . . . They are no longer two people, you see, but forms and colours, forms and colours that have taken on, meanwhile, the idea of two people and preserve the vibration of their life."

Many readers skipped Picasso's words and interpreted the title in the more obvious way, one that still makes us both cringe. "They are no longer two people, they are one." No matter how much we were wallowing in the throes of passion, we didn't want to melt together into one sticky mess. We both worked hard to keep our separate selves intact. I wish we'd used instead a quotation by Rilke: "I hold this to be the highest task for a bond between two people: that each protects the solitude of the other." But then what would we have called the book? Maybe *The Highest Task*? That sounds quasi-religious, overblown. Maybe *Two Solitudes*? But in Canada that title's been used and used well.

We launched *No Longer Two People* in the spring of 1979 at St. John's College in Winnipeg. Sandra Birdsell, who'd started publishing stories in magazines and who, along with me, was a member of a small writing group, approached us after the reading and asked how we could strip naked in front of an audience. We'd thought we'd disguised ourselves fairly well, the poems redolent with images from nature and loaded with archetypes, shadows of the animus and anima (we'd been reading Jung at the time), and each piece was as well crafted as we could make it. Our lives appeared in the details for sure, but we didn't see the dialogue as an exposé. We thought we were exploring how to write about love when both lovers were poets. It hadn't been done before, as far as we knew, this litany for two voices written with the flesh but also, we'd hoped, with the intellect.

It was the first and last time we'd collaborate—not because of Sandra's reaction, though it was echoed by others, but because it felt dangerous to walk that explosive line between autobiography and aestheticism, to braid our shared experiences and our art together in so direct and unflinching a way. How could a couple survive that? Our words and many of our daily practices would continue to interweave, but we sang solo after that, not as part of a duet. Is that one of the compacts that has kept us together for forty years? I don't know.

Patrick was the more resistant about working in tandem again. Though his poems and novels come from things that he's going through, most of his writing digs deeper into his past. I'm the opposite. A lot of what inspires me is shorter-fused—it could flare from something recent—and he's never acclimatized to how a conversation we have today might appear in a poem tomorrow. If I want to be the kind of writer I am, I have to ignore his unease around my use of our daily exchanges and actions as starter fuel. Otherwise I'd have a censor on my shoulder, and I'd be unable to put anything down on paper. It hasn't been easy, though, negotiating between intimacy and inspiration, between autobiography and disguise. The bargain I've struck with myself is that I ask him, when I write something that involves our shared particulars in a way that's thinly camouflaged, if I can send the piece out for publication or if I should just drop it in a drawer.

About twenty years ago, I wrote three poems about a very difficult aspect of our lives: his alcoholism and its effects on me. I was afraid to go there, but I couldn't stop the words from fracturing the silence that glassed in those troubling hours we shared. I showed him the poems after I'd made them the best they could be and said, "Do you want me to toss these?" He fell quiet after he read them. Then he said, "No, they're good. Send them out." We never talked about the content, the unhappiness of the speaker, who was me. We never talked about the deterioration of our relationship, the poems small alarm bells going off. It took three years after their publication in *What the Living Won't Let Go* for Patrick to choose to be sober. It had nothing to do with poetry. It had nothing to do with love.

WALKING INTO THE FUTURE

Months after, your mother's death is
something you pull on every morning,
old flannel tight across your chest.
It's been a hard year—your drinking, stopping,
stopping again, and I've been on the road
too much. Learned a distance I didn't know
before, a space that separates one
phone call, one city from the next. Still
everything continues, including love,
including loneliness. It's the same
house we live in. The same tree
stains our deck with yellow plums
predictable in late July. Wasps feast

on this sweet mating with the sun.
What changes? Lately there are things
I do not tell you—I ache inside, you
sadden me. Away too long I carry
my bags up the front steps to our porch,
hesitate as I've never done before.
Sun-blind, I walk into the future,
see only shapes—a couch, a chair,
and someone rising. I don't know who
you will be.

April, 2017

PATRICK AND I have been cabined, cribbed, confined for months on end. We've had to cancel so many things at the last minute: family dinners, theatre dates and concerts, literary events. There's no way to predict the day before or even the morning of the gathering whether Patrick will have the strength to go out. I can't remember when we last sat together at a friend's table, our eyes warm with the sight of familiar faces, our ears buzzing with good talk.

Things we'd normally enjoy together, I've been attending solo. I launched my new book at Munro's in Victoria with him not there, received the George Woodcock Lifetime Achievement Award at the Vancouver Public Library with his absence palpable in the room, performed in his stead at a provincial Master Gardeners conference in Sidney, the town closest to where we live. There, I read from his memoir set in the garden of our former house and concluded the time allotted to him with his poem that ends "Tonight I took my shorn hair and laid it on the arms of the pines. / In the morning the hummingbirds will line their nests with me." As I came to the last few words, all the air in the room became one massive inhalation from hundreds of gardeners. It was released in what sounded like a single sigh.

I feel honoured to be speaking for Patrick but I can't help but wonder if my appearances as a single woman when we'd normally be together are a rehearsal for what's to come. When I arrive at a party unaccompanied, when I sit by myself in the dark of the cinema because Patrick can't make it to the movie we both want to see, am I practicing loneliness? Will anything help prepare me for his not being by my side? I can't let myself think about it.

I discovered in my mid-twenties, when I began writing and publishing, that poems are more prescient than any fortune teller. The lyrics in my debut collection announced the end of my first marriage before I knew it was over. I would have argued that the central persona was a fictional character. (Didn't she have children, for instance, while I didn't? Wasn't she a baker of bread while I'd never made a loaf in my life?) This woman felt trapped and wanted out. I did too, but it took me almost a decade to admit that I longed to detonate the life I'd settled on at twenty when I walked down the aisle in a long white dress and changed my name from Crozier to Uher. What was I thinking? Less than two years after saying my vows, I yearned to be free and dangerous and on the run. Before I found the courage to throw a match on this nascent desire, the poems smouldered with my unhappiness, my thwarted self. What do my poems say now? If I read them with a distant eye, what future would I read?

A couple of years ago, as a fundraiser for the Writers' Union of Canada, the writer and actor Chris Humphreys organized a reading on his home island of Salt Spring, featuring himself and another resident, Kathy Page, as well as my old friend Bill Deverell and me. We were invited to read what we'd left on the editing room floor. Kathy and Bill delighted the audience with amusing bits of excess from their fiction, Chris from an early play: passages they'd cut before the prose went into print or onto a stage. I didn't have anything, not because I don't write dreck and hopefully excise it, but because I don't keep it around. I drop my various versions in boxes for an archive and delete the files from my computer. Without any example of egregious writing close at hand, I decided to read a poem from my first collection, a small chapbook called *Inside Is the Sky.* I was in my mid-twenties, a wife for four years bearing my husband's name, and I'd just been bitten by the poetry bug. The poem I read to the crowd ended like this:

> Her lipmarks remain on the rim of her coffee cup
> and the smooth surface of his forehead,
> but she unwrapped her brain
> rolled in wax-paper, dated and filed in the freezer.
>
> She has crept
> through the caragana jungle.
> She has trampled through the heads of wheat.
> She has leapt aboard a moving train
> bound for Toronto.
> "One way to Toronto, please."
> One way
> to a disappearance.

I'm fond of that young writer, of her overstatement, her resounding feminist anger, her desire to create booming metaphor. I'm also tickled by the destination for her great escape—Toronto! It was a place that, at that time, I'd never been, and it was as far from

Saskatchewan as I could imagine going. Looking back, I feel sorry for that young writer's husband, who read those early barometers of my unhappiness before I was able to face it. It's no wonder he said, "Why do you write this shit?" It's no wonder I had to get out.

The twenty-two-year-old chemistry honours student who fell in love with me at university didn't end up with what he'd bargained for. Without talking about it, I'd promised him one kind of woman and turned into another. At eighteen, when I started sneaking out of the women's residence after curfew to meet him, I was an uncultured small-town girl whose education was going to be a ticket out of the poverty I'd grown up with. The first person in my extended family to go to university, I wanted a profession that would give me a good salary, that would last for years, and that would generate a decent pension when I retired. Strangely, at least as far as I can remember, in the decade we were together, we didn't consider having children. Was that because, based on my childhood, I didn't find family life a source of happiness? My prime goal was to be independent and to pay my own way. I didn't want to end up like my mom, who I'd watch beg my father for grocery money. He'd slide a five dollar bill across the Arborite kitchen table and as she'd reach for it, he'd sweep it back and palm it until she'd ask again.

After my first degree, with majors in psychology and English literature, I fell into teaching because it was the only career I knew that had any connection with those two specialties and because it took only an extra eight months to get a professional certificate that would land me a position. Putting myself through school with summer jobs and scholarships, I couldn't afford any more years of study. When I started to think of poetry as something I needed to stay alive, the edges of my marriage began to fray. It wasn't long before it tore easily apart in my fingers where I'd been picking at the seams.

My writing life began after my husband and I found jobs in my hometown, Swift Current, Saskatchewan. It wasn't where I wanted to be. There, my father was infamous. He'd lost his license several times, had been driven home by the police, had spent nights in the drunk tank. Until I left home at eighteen, I had lived in shame and fear and poverty, but the southwest school district was the only one in the province that offered positions to both of us. We'd resigned from our first teaching posts in a small school in Glaslyn, in the north of the province. The principal, who'd become a friend, had warned us that the board wanted us gone.

Though in Glaslyn I'd discovered I loved teaching and we'd been happy our two years there, we'd stirred things up. It was 1972. I taught *Jesus Christ Superstar* and the lyrics of Bob Dylan, Leonard Cohen, and Joni Mitchell as poetry in my grade ten and eleven classrooms. I wore miniskirts and purple suede platform heels bought in Gastown in Vancouver when we visited friends there in the summer. My husband had a beard and long hair, we drove a foreign car, we didn't have children, and some of the townspeople thought we poured too much affection into our dog, who wasn't a farm mutt but a purebred beagle. We'd also demanded at a public forum that the school board buy typewriters and art supplies so that students who couldn't master the more difficult classes like chemistry and physics would have others to choose from and would be able to cobble together enough credits to graduate. With righteous fervour, my husband argued openly with the Chair of the school board in a room crowded with parents and wouldn't let her off the hook. I knew by the look on her face that we were in trouble.

In Swift Current, his new job would be to teach science in junior high and mine to teach grades ten through twelve literature and composition, what we called English then. I was always an avid reader but I'd started to write poems that I didn't show anyone. Something inchoate was stirring inside me, something I had to find words for, though I couldn't have said what that craving meant or why it began more and more to occupy my inner life like seep inside a dirt-walled cellar.

What set me firmly on my poetic path when I was twenty-four years old was Ken Mitchell's visit to the high school where I taught. Ken, a professor at the University of Regina, was a playwright and short-story writer. I don't remember who invited him, but I was a fan and I'd typed out and mimeographed his short story "The Great Electrical Revolution" to teach to my grade ten class. So much for copyright! I didn't even think about it.

Ken's task was to inspire the eight of us in the English Department to incorporate creative writing into our curriculum. Before he arrived, he gave us homework: we were each to write a poem and send it to him in Regina. I struggled with one about my Welsh grandfather, who'd beaten my mother with a willow switch as she scuttled out of reach under the bed she shared with six siblings in their cramped house on the farm. This was the same man who'd been nothing but gentle with me when I was a child. The poem tells the story through the point of view of a little girl led into the barn by her grandfather, her hand in his. In the muted light that barely makes it through the dust-smeared windows, he shows her how to speak to the pair of work horses that tower above her in the stalls and stamp the wooden floor with huge hooves.

I didn't know if the poem was good or bad. What I did know was how much I'd loved writing it, how much I'd turned over every syllable, read each draft out loud, cut and polished and tried to breathe life into the words. I also knew that the source of inspiration for me was something that resisted language, something I didn't understand—in this case, the disturbing double nature of my grandfather. Somehow I knew this fraught place of no-words-for-it was the territory where poetry began. I couldn't wait for Ken's visit to our school. It was the first time I was going to meet a flesh-and-blood writer, not only that, but someone who lived in my own province. It was the first time a craftsman who knew what he was doing was going to cast his eye over my words.

Ken walked into the library at the high school on a Friday afternoon after the students had gone home. The hallways held the kind of silence that only the absence of hundreds of teenagers can bring. With my colleagues—six men and one other woman—I sat at a long table in front of stacks of books. Ken carried a battered leather briefcase, a common prop of cool university professors. He dressed like them too, blue jeans and a denim shirt, his feet in hiking boots. His skin was the kind that would burn and peel in a prairie summer. I guessed he was in his mid-thirties, about ten years older than me.

A published, working writer, a member of a species I'd encountered only on the page, but he could have been someone from my childhood, a buddy of my older brother. A hockey player at our local rink, a farm boy who banged down the tail gate of an old pickup so he and his pals could perch there and tip back bottles of beer.

He started his session by saying he was going to go through each of our poems, critiquing them the way he would if they'd come to *Grain*, Saskatchewan's new literary magazine, where he was one of the founding editors. He wouldn't read out the name on the poem, and he didn't know who anyone was in the room; we could break our anonymity if we wanted to, but for now, it was our words and his editor's eye. There was nothing personal about it. My colleague beside me shifted in his chair. I let out a breath. I wondered if his goal was to put us in our students' shoes, to show us how vulnerable we'd feel when it was our writing on the line. Was he trying to show us that it wasn't easy? That he didn't get where he was because it was easy?

Ken wasn't cruel, but he didn't hold back. He pointed out one or two things that were working, sometimes having to stretch to get there, but then he tore into the sentimentality, the vagueness, the overstatement, the summative endings. Why did this poem sound like Wordsworth, three centuries later? Why was this one chock full of allusions that only an Eliot could pull off? I became more and more nervous as he got closer to the end of the pile, colleague after colleague gamely claiming what they'd written, joking about their small humiliations.

I'd told none of my co-workers that I read poetry not just for pleasure or to find something I thought my students would like, but to learn what poets knew about line and diction and form. As Ken went through each submission, I was preparing to be cool, clever, ironic when my turn came. I would act as nonchalant as the others—this was just a little thing, a learning experience that wouldn't wound something deep inside. We were at the table to be better teachers, not better writers. After all, that's what we were: high school teachers, not poets. Not would-be spinners of stories on a page.

Suddenly there was no one left but me. My poem would be the last. I waited to hear Ken's voice read the words I'd written. But nothing happened. "That's it," Ken said. "Time for a break."

For the rest of the day, Ken took us through what he was looking for in a good piece of writing and showed how we could get that across to our students. He'd brought in books by Alden Nowlan and Al Purdy and Raymond Souster, and by Anne Szumigalski, whom he worked with at *Grain*. I had never heard of her before and, at this point, I was only half listening. At the end of his session

I mustered the courage to approach him and ask why he'd decided to leave my poem out. Was it so bad he'd set it aside? He said, "What was your name again?" When I told him, he paused. "I didn't receive anything from you. It must've gotten lost."

"That's okay," I said, both relieved and disappointed. I grabbed my coat and papers and felt grateful I could lower my head to search my purse for my keys.

"Look," he said, "if you want to send it to me, go ahead. I'll look at it and give you a response."

"Sure," I said, "I'll do that." But I wouldn't. I could tell he was being kind, he wasn't interested. Why would he be? Nothing I'd said that morning would have made me stand out, would have caught his eye. I felt ashamed of my ambitions. I felt small.

When I got home my husband, who was outside changing the oil in our truck, asked, "How'd it go?" He knew how important the day had been to me.

"He didn't get my poem." I opened the door to the house, called the dog and clipped the leash to her collar. "I'll just take her for a walk," I said, as if it didn't matter. "I'll start supper after."


Although my mother grew proud of my achievements as a writer, she had no idea where this strange poetry part of me came from. Nor did I. I was born into a family of ordinary, hard-working Saskatchewan people who had grown up on farms across the road from one another, my father quitting school in grade eight to help with the harvest and seeding and chores, taking over more responsibility for those tasks after the death of his father. Despite the years of work he put in, he lost the farm to his younger brother when his mother died ten years after his father. She'd always treated her younger son better than her elder—who knows why?

Just after my brother was born, seven years before me, my parents moved with their new baby to the small town of Success, only ten miles or so from the farms where they'd grown up, and squatted in an abandoned railroad car near the tracks. Dad laboured in nearby fields as a hired hand. It must have been hard on him, being a paid labourer for neighbours who'd expected him to have his own land to work. My parents soon moved again, thirty miles away to a wreckedy rental house in the city of Swift Current, where Dad drove a backhoe in the oil patch and was laid off in the winter when the ground froze. The loss of the land, my mom said, and the hurt his mother had inflicted, triggered his drinking. I know now that alcoholism is more complicated than that, but at the time her reasoning made as much sense as anything.

My father always had enough money to drink in the bars every night and to buy toys for himself without consulting my mother, including a speed boat with a big Evinrude motor; but when his boss let him go during the coldest season, my parents' worry about paying the rent thickened the air. I could hear it in their anger over what seemed to be minor things, like my mother folding my father's handkerchiefs badly before she stuffed them in his bottom drawer, or Dad's delay in fixing the bedroom closet door that hung on one hinge. It was impossible for my brother and me to deflect their irritation and anxiety. Against my father's wishes—no wife of his would work—my mother said "Just watch me" like some domestic Dirty Harry and marched out the door to find ways to earn her own money. I was in grade one and my brother in grade eight. She became a housecleaner, a lowly job then, for the wife of one of the lawyers who lived in a cluster of new expensive homes on top of the hill. Sometimes her work included watching over three little kids while she cleaned, and sometimes the woman who employed her didn't have cash and asked her to wait a week to get paid. Her salary was a dollar an hour.

Soon she found a summer job as a basket checker and cashier at the outdoor swimming pool. That was a good thing for me because to keep me in her sight and to avoid having to pay for a sitter, she enrolled me in lessons, and at eight years old I learned to swim, spending hours at the pool just two blocks up the alley from our house. By grade eleven, I'd become a lifeguard, the best June to September job for a teenager in our town and a good way to meet boys. I paraded around the cement apron of the pool, getting paid to get a tan. The smell of chlorine on my skin carries me back to those combustible, hot months of early adolescence, the baby-oiled gleam of my young body in a Speedo swimsuit, a silver whistle strung around my neck.

In winter when the pool was boarded up, my mother sold tickets at the hockey games. They were harder to get to. The Swift Current Broncos played their hometown games at the civic centre, an ugly cinderblock cube on the edge of the city about an hour's trek from where we lived. My mother had never learned to drive. Because she couldn't count on my father to be sober or on time, she headed off into the dark alone, trudging through the snow, a small, bundled-up woman leaning into the wind and its whips of cold, visible only in the bright pools cast by the streetlamps and the narrow beams of headlights. She became a familiar figure in our town, often the only pedestrian on the streets at night. If she was offered a ride, she'd refuse. Out of pride, she'd say she liked to walk, not wanting anyone to know our family secret—her husband was a drunk and she couldn't depend on him to drive her. Surely no one believed that she chose to traipse through the chill and dark as a recreational pastime before and after she sold tickets, but what could they do? She'd thank whoever stopped on the side of the road for their kindness and keep on going.

BLIZZARD

Walking into wind, I lean into my mother's muskrat coat;
around the cuffs her wristbones have worn away the fur.

If we stood still we'd disappear. There's no up or down,
no houses with their windows lit. The only noise is wind

and what's inside us. When we get home my father
will be there or not. No one ever looks for us.

I could lie down and stay right here where snow is all
that happens, and silence isn't loneliness just cold

not talking. My mother tugs at me and won't let go.
Then stops to find her bearings. In our hoods of stars

we don't know if anyone will understand
the tongue we speak, so far we are from home.

Though I don't remember ever going hungry, poverty—not just the financial kind—was always a presence in our house, like an infestation of bed bugs you knew were there even when they scuttled out of sight. My parents' family farms were both bleak and treeless outposts, void of anything that wasn't of daily use, including any riches or beauty that the arts can bring. One exception, though they were certainly practical and used nightly on every bed, were the quilts my grandmothers jigsawed from patches cut from hand-me-down clothes, the fabric worn so thin there were more holes than cloth. I loved to lie on them when we visited, run my fingers over the smooth or nubby squares and make up stories of imaginary people who'd once looked so fine.

Neither my father nor my mother had grown up with pianos or paintings or books promising other possibilities beyond the drought-stricken fields, the mean and shabby rooms. That paucity of fine things continued into my childhood home. The walls of our house sported only one painting—a silhouetted deer against the backdrop of a mountain and waterfall, created by a nomadic artist named Flexhaug who roamed the prairies to sell his work—every piece essentially the same—on street corners, often outside of bars. My father bought it in front of the York Hotel on Central Avenue for five bucks. He was proud of it and liked to look at it. "That guy knew how to paint," he said.

I wish I'd talked to him about it—his nascent appreciation of what he saw as talent, his love of what he saw as beauty. Maybe I would have understood a side of him I never got close to. Maybe I'd have felt fond of that part of him that longed for something else, something that reached beyond the dry monotony of the farmland where he'd grown up, beyond his family's betrayal and the daily grind of his and my mother's lives. That painting now hangs in the hall beside the room Patrick and I have turned into a library. I didn't have to fight my brother for it—he didn't share my affection for those simple brush strokes on cheap particle board. I've had it framed so that you can see the holes in the four corners where my father pounded it frameless into the living room wall.

Another part of my father I missed out on was his love of playing the fiddle. Though not a member of any band, Mom said he often picked up the instrument at the school dances in the town hall and, self-taught, he'd saw out the tunes for a quick foxtrot.

They both loved to dance and found a home in each other's arms when the music was playing. He sold the fiddle shortly after I was born to buy a big combination radio-record player. Dark and shiny, it loomed in the living room as important as a family shrine. On top of it sat a doily that had been part of my mother's trousseau and a plastic vase of plastic roses. One day when I was four, I hit the front of the varnished wood with a stick again and again—I couldn't have explained why. After snatching me away and scolding me, Mom covered the scratches with a brown crayon so my father wouldn't see. He never spanked me or even yelled at me—but what behaviour might have been prompted by such a sacrilege if he'd found out? Scared but gleeful, I knew I had done something very bad.

There were only about ten records in my parents' collection, stored in the space below the turntable, but the dial on the big radio was set to CKSW Swift Current, its country music twanging through the rooms. Their favourite was a program called "The Tractor Line." Before farmers and their wives headed out to the fields, they'd request a tune that the host, Art Wallman, would play when they were harrowing or seeding or hauling grain. If there was a celebrity in Swift Current, it was Art. "Got a call from Murray out near Hazlet. He's wanting Wilf Carter's 'There's a Love Knot in My Lariat' for his wife, Eileen. It was the song they danced to when they met. Hope that knot is holding fast." By the time I was a teenager, I turned up my nose at the corny words and songs and dedications. When I was younger, I sang along.

Our family library was as paltry as the art and music collection. In its entirety it fit into a wooden apple crate standing on one end in the front hall. I don't know where my parents found such a box, apples being a rarity in Saskatchewan, but Dad had wedged a plank in the middle for a second shelf. Until they bought a bedroom suite shortly after I was born, the apple box functioned as my mother's dresser. She'd painted it peppermint pink, and it stayed that colour when it mutated into a repository for the family's scant volumes. On the lower level rose a stack of my brother's comic books. They changed and the numbers accumulated, spilling out of the space because he traded one for two with the other kids on the block every Saturday morning. I worshipped my older brother for his cleverness, his courage around bullies, and his prowess at the hockey rink; but mostly for his ability to regenerate and expand his stash of Superman, Captain Marvel, the Lone Ranger, and Rex the Wonderdog. The succinct language, the onomatopoeic *Boom, Shebang, Crash!* planted in me the first seeds of poetry. How could words be so delicious, so noisy, so rich?

Above the comics on the top shelf sat the books that no one even tried to trade and that stayed the same. Along with a dictionary my brother lifted from his seventh-grade classroom and the Bible my mom received from the Anglican church when she took First Communion, there were three hardcovers—one volume of *The Book of Knowledge*, Sir Walter Scott's *The Bride of Lammermoor*, its corners chewed by mice, and only the spine and covers of Zane Grey's *Code of the West*. I grew up wondering where the pages had gone and what that code might be.

After I started publishing, the library in my parents' house exploded because I, and then Patrick, sent them books. In their mid-sixties, they finally owned their own house, bought for $6,000 with my maternal grandfather's help. Instead of paying fifty bucks a month for rent to the slum landlord who lived in a beautiful character home across the street from the small run-down duplex we'd moved to when I was fourteen, they paid my grandfather. My mother was the last of his six living children he helped, though she was the only one who did anything for him.

Every Saturday, for years after my grandmother died and he'd moved into town from the farm, my mother walked to his small house a few blocks away, picked up his laundry and cleaned his rooms, scrubbing with all her might to eradicate the ochre streaks from the chewing tobacco he spat into the toilet. If he needed groceries, she got them, too, and though she didn't drink, she'd stop at the liquor store and pick up a bottle of cheap brandy that he kept on the floor by his bed. He claimed a shot every morning was what propelled his feet out of the covers and onto the cold linoleum even when he was well into his nineties. On Sundays she brought back his clothes, clean and ironed and neatly folded.

Doing my grandfather's laundry wasn't easy work for her. The washing machine was an old wringer in the dirt cellar of the duplex. On wash day, which always fell on a Monday, water gathered in a scummy pool on the floor because the drains were bad. Past the washing machine was the toilet, with a half wall of plywood my dad had nailed on the side open to the low-ceilinged cellar. I tried to use it less on Mondays, because I hated getting my feet wet. Even in winter, Mom hung the clothes outside on the line. When she brought them in, hard and stiff as if the cold and frost had been spiked with starch, she draped them on chairs in front of the stove. My grandfather's long white underwear looked like a headless ghost I should sneak past so it wouldn't spring into action and grab me.

In the first house my parents owned, the apple crate had settled into a corner in the basement—not a cellar this time, but a real basement with cement walls and floors, the books on its shelves giving way to jars of saskatoon jam and chokecherry jelly. The pride of place in the living room was taken up by a two-tiered maple coffee table my brother and I bought them for their fortieth wedding anniversary. On the bottom level of the polished table my mother piled, in two neat rows, Patrick's and my books. It was lucky they were poetry; they were thin, and no matter how many we sent over the years—there must have been thirty or so by the time she died—they took up little room.

On the top of the same table crouched a big plastic lobster my father had brought back from a visit to my brother, who was stationed in PEI as a helicopter search-and-rescue pilot. Mom and Dad waved at every helicopter that thrummed overhead in Swift Current, hoping that, like a homing pigeon, he was returning to Saskatchewan. Neither of my parents would eat the crustaceans when they stayed with him and his family on the island, but my father couldn't get over the fact that Maritimers, including his son, daughter-in-law, and three grandkids, cracked them open and devoured the pale meat, chins shiny with melted butter. The orange lobster squatted in its place of honour above our volumes of poetry until my father died and my mom got rid of it. Our books remained.

Sixteen years later, after my mother died and before the house was sold, I stacked the books in one of the cardboard boxes I'd picked up from the liquor store. I bet my mom could have boasted the biggest library on the street. Certainly the biggest poetry collection in the entire city. In the days of packing up her things, I'd donated or tossed so much, including dozens of curling trophies with *Peggy Crozier* or *Emerson Crozier* engraved on a small plaque underneath a bronze man or woman holding a broom. I didn't know what to do with the books, all dedicated to her with sentimental salutations. I can't remember now if we signed them for my father, too, the years he was alive. Maybe not—he read nothing but the *Swift Current Sun*, following the lines of print with his finger. But all the *Dear Mom*s brought her close, and magnified how much I would miss her. How much I would miss this woman who said she didn't understand my poetry but wanted it around even when I wrote about my father without pity and with little affection. In a book published ten years after her death and twenty-six years after his, I wrote a poem about him that I think she would have liked. Maybe he would have, too.

OLD STYLE

*Count the crows,* my father said,
on the Old Style Pilsner label,
*then the rabbits.* One, two, three—
I loved the beer smell of his breath
as he whisker-rubbed my cheeks—four!
*Oh, you're the clever one,* he said.

There were also Indians, a red jalopy,
a biplane with a rabbit in the pilot's seat,
and a train, grey smudge above the smokestack.
These days, I ride it to get back, press my cheek
against the glass, watch everything slip by so fast.

Tonight it's winter, the train's unheated.
The bottle's frosted around the lip
as if sipped by moonlight. Up ahead
I glimpse a man at a station, boarded-up.

He's small enough to be my father
standing there, swinging a lantern
against the cold, snow falling all around him
so I can barely see. The train won't stop.
*Count the crows,* he said, and I count them still.

## June, 2017

WE'RE HALFWAY TO the doctor's office, the hematologist this time, when Patrick has me turn around and go back to our starting point. He's seen a spider hanging from a thread from his window on the passenger's side and he wants to return it to our yard. "It might not make it in the city," he says. "We have to take it home."

Patrick has an inordinate love of spiders. I learned from him that if I don't want one in the house, I don't stamp on it and smash it flat as my mother, proud housekeeper that she was, would have done. I slide it onto a piece of paper and carry it outside. If it were up to him, our rooms would be sighing with webs. He's on the poet Issa's side: "Don't worry, spiders, / I keep house / casually." I delight with him when I come upon their handiwork in the fall, strung between the shrubs and pearled with dew. I lean in, seeing with his near-sighted eyes the big female pluck her strings at the centre of her web. We stand still and silent, as if she can hear us, and follow the male spider's attempt to approach her to mate, his brave, eight-footed dance inching him toward her. There's a quick collision, then a stillness, and a commotion as he flees. When he leaps to the outside edge of the trembling circle, we can see he's lost a leg but he's survived, managing to scuttle away from this dangerous encounter and bungee jump to the leaves below.

Sometimes Patrick catches flies with a backward swoop of his hand and drops them in the gossamer spokes if he worries the spider is going hungry. In doing so, he's paying obeisance to one of the household and garden gods, spinner, storyteller, wisdom-keeper. In the world of the Lakota, many of whom we played baseball with during the weeks we taught at the summer school in the Qu'Appelle Valley, spider hatched from a great cosmic egg laid by the thunderstorm. He gave the people language. Perhaps that's why he's a trickster figure who mixes folly with wisdom, a paradox writers understand. Patrick has sensed that link between himself and arachnids, as he spins his words across a page.

"I measure friendship by those who are friends of spiders and those who are not," he writes in his memoir. "To me there is nothing more beautiful than an orb weaver as she makes her web in the early evening in anticipation of tomorrow's feasting. Watching her slow, patient dance as she moves in ever-decreasing circles from the perimeter, pausing at each of the walking strings to anchor her catching-silk. The sticky silk radiates inward in a spiral like a star that is going nova. Rise with the dawn and count the dream-catchers in your garden. You will find them by their jewelled webs festooned with a thousand droplets of dew. The first rays of the sun as they break above the far mountains catch their many webs and turns them into the purest form of meditation there is."

Two months after my encounter with the writer Ken Mitchell at the high school where I taught, my husband dropped a pile of mail on the kitchen table. A power bill, a subscription notice for *Time*, a letter from a childhood friend who lived in Saskatoon, and an envelope with a return address in Germany. I opened it last. It was from Ken. "Strange thing. I'm on sabbatical in Hamburg and among the papers I brought to work on, I found your poem with your address. I like it. If you're okay with this, I'm giving it to the other editors of *Grain*. If they like it, too, we'll publish it."

And that was the start of it. It was then I knew that poetry would be something I would do all my life. What did I mean when I said that, resoundingly, to myself, telling no one else? It was just one poem and not very good. Did I know that poetry—which someone of note had just affirmed I could write with some skill, however embryonic—more than anything else made me pay rapt attention to the world and was therefore something rare and precious? It was poetry that rubbed away the cynicism I'd already begun to gather around my being, though I was only twenty-four, poetry that shrunk the distance between who I was and who I wanted to be. I didn't figure it out then or pronounce it, but it was poetry that led me to first words, first sounds, first heartache and first love, first hands placed upon the earth. It was poetry that changed and charged me.

It came from and returned me to that artless kid who knelt for hours in the dirt watching a string of ants each carrying an egg like a round, white syllable to their nest under the earth, spelling something out in the loamy darkness; that kid who saw a likeness between a bluebird and a scrap of prairie sky and who felt what could only be called exaltation when she wrote across the page in a line or two what happened when her eyes met the eyes of a fox in the wild grass near the railway tracks. *Boom! Crash! Shebang!*

In his letter Ken went on to tell me he taught a three-week workshop in July at the Saskatchewan Summer School of the Arts. It was located in what used to be a TB sanitarium outside of the town of Fort Qu'Appelle, about forty-five minutes east of Regina. If I wanted to study there, he wrote, he'd accept me. Anne Szumigalski was on the faculty and the novelist and poet Robert Kroetsch would be coming up from Binghamton, New York. I'd never heard of him, but since Ken had mentioned Anne during the workshop in Swift Current, I'd found her book, *Woman Reading in Bath*. I didn't understand everything but I loved the flightiness of her imagination, her eccentricity and charming wickedness. The poems were bawdy but with a British reticence—she was raised in a village outside of London—and salted with an oddness that was entirely her own. I couldn't believe she was a housewife with four children, as her biographical note said, one daughter born the year before me. And she lived in my province, in Saskatoon.

At the time I'd been reading another Anne, the American poet Anne Sexton. In the photographs I came across in one of the magazines at the library—was it *Life* or *Time*?—she posed model-slim and sophisticated in high heels and a tight black skirt, a cigarette pinched between manicured, tapered fingers. This, I thought, was the figure of a woman poet—a movie star from a script written by Dashiell Hammett. I imagined this Saskatchewan Anne would be equally as glamorous. She'd be a woman of martinis and dark basement clubs and yellow taxis swishing with big-city purpose through the rain.

Three months after hearing from Ken, my husband drove me to the clutch of former sanitarium buildings in the verdant valley of the Qu'Appelle River. It was four hours and a universe from Swift Current. In the back seat squatted the blue vinyl suitcase my mother had given me for my grade twelve graduation, and a second-hand typewriter I'd found in a storage room at the school. It was so heavy it could have sunk a cow in a dugout. One key, the *d*, stuck. I was a bad, slow typist, so it didn't matter. I could take the time to unstick it. At least it wasn't a vowel, especially an *e*. If it really bothered me, I could abandon any words with *d*. I could substitute *melancholy* for *depressed*, *canine* for *dog*, *father* for *dad*, *lit to the gills* for *drunk*.

Before I left home, I spent an hour in the school library and read about the place where I was going. Though my husband had grown up in Regina, less than an hour away, he'd never been there and knew nothing about it. The summer school nestled in the oasis-like Qu'Appelle Valley, blessed with four lakes and shadowed by a rich and tragic history. At Fort Qu'Appelle, the biggest town in the valley's two-hundred-mile stretch and the former Hudson's Bay post, the most important treaty of western Canada was signed by the Cree, Saulteaux, and Assiniboine in 1874. Treaty 4 ceded a whopping 75,000 square miles of territory, mostly in present-day southern Saskatchewan, to the Crown in exchange for promises that were soon broken. Shortly after, Sitting Bull's people, torn from their land and starving, sought sanctuary after the Battle of the Little Bighorn in 1881 and were refused; the Oblate Fathers built the first residential school in the West in the nearby town of Lebret in 1884; and thirty-three years later, in 1917, a few miles to the north of the fort and on the shores of Echo Lake, buildings were constructed to house 350 patients, all of them sick and many of them dying of TB. Called Fort San, it was reinvented as a summer school of the arts in 1967, a few patients still on site.

My husband helped me carry my stuff to the room I'd been assigned in the former staff residence where the TB nurses once stayed. In the back of the complex, behind the other buildings, it functioned as the writers' centre. On two floors there were rooms with single beds and tiny desks, and what had once been the lounge on the main level would host the workshops. He hugged me and said he'd be back to pick me up in three weeks. I didn't want him to leave. I waved at his tall frame behind the wheel, the car diminishing second by second, the tires spewing gravel and dust, then I walked across the vast lawns in front of the four low-slung pavilions used as dorms, mainly for the hundreds of music students. Big as cruise ships, they boasted screened verandahs where staff for five decades had wheeled the invalids for fresh air. These buildings had more character than the utilitarian, squat writers' lodge—they seemed grounded, doomed, washed ashore by the storms of a violent past.

I'd like to say that those who came to know the valley, including me, felt the chill of its history when we arrived to study there. In the mid-seventies, though, I didn't know anything about that history, at least the Indigenous part. I don't feel good saying that. Like everyone I knew, I was ignorant of residential schools and the horrific abuse that had gone on there. I probably thought of the "*first* residential school in the West," situated in my home province, as a source of pride, as the first place that offered Indigenous kids an education that would improve their lives. Never had I heard the words "cultural genocide." Or "stolen children." Nor was I familiar with the Cree word for schools such as this: *kiskinwa-hamctowikamik*—a building you go to to learn to cry.

The old red-brick building in Lebret—the locals called it "the Indian School"—looked deceptively charming in its surround of trees. I visited its grounds only once and never went back. For those of us who dropped into the valley for a brief time to write, the boarded-up historical building wasn't the town's focal point. That was the folksy bar with its shuffleboard, pickled eggs in a round-bellied glass jar, and big dusty windows that stared placidly at the narrow lake where pelicans landed with the weight and grace of falling angels.

We did, though, feel traces of other lives in the sanitarium's grounds where we worked long hours and slept and swapped stories, some of us for several summers, and where thousands of patients over its twenty-four-year span had wasted away, hoping for a cure for the terrible disease that had smitten them. Many of them were Indigenous. Many, no matter what their race, age, or background, never returned to their families, but died far from home and the comfort of their loved ones. No one doubted that this deep declivity carved by glaciers had been a place of illness and suffering and that spirits found it difficult to leave. Once you studied there, you found it difficult to leave, too. The ghostly part of it held an uncanny allure. In more ways than one, it was haunted.

Two winters after my first stay at the school, my husband bought me a typewriter for Christmas. It was a portable turquoise Smith Corona. I was shocked when I tore the wrapping paper off the box—how much had it cost him to give me this? By then, my writing was pulling me further and further away. I had a new group of friends he wasn't a part of. I went to readings and book launches and parties alone. I was having an affair with an older writer who taught at the summer school—it had started that first year, and I didn't think my husband knew. After unwrapping all the presents at his parents' house in Regina, he'd followed me upstairs into the bathroom, the only place we could be alone. I couldn't get over his goodness, his generosity. Overwhelmed with guilt, I sat on the edge of the tub and cried. "I'm sorry I'm so hard to live with," I said. "I'm sorry you're so hard to live without," he replied.

After he drove away from Fort San that first summer, in the central courtyard where I sat under one of the big spruces, the late afternoon breeze, cool off the lake, carried the sound of brass and string instruments from the practice halls, and several young women, taut-bodied, obviously part of the dance classes, strode gracefully past, hair knotted on top of their small perfect heads, the long ribbons of their satin shoes draped over their shoulders. They were ten years younger than me, in their early- to mid-adolescence, but they looked confident, sophisticated, as if they'd spent time at finishing schools in Switzerland and France. No doubt they spoke three languages. I didn't belong there. I was scared. I felt ignorant and inept. Although I was twenty-four and had been a wife for four years, this would be the first time since my marriage that I'd sleep in a bed without my husband beside me. Three weeks of being on my own.

As I tried to breathe calmly, to talk myself into not running to the road and hitching a ride to the highway and home, a huge woman in a loose floral dress drifted toward me like a figure from Fellini, whose movies I'd seen at the foreign film society at university. I couldn't help but stare. In spite of her size, she floated across the lawn as if someone had glued wings above her heels. Long grey hair, uncombed and tangled, stormed behind her. When she got closer she peered at me through thick glasses, her eyes magnified, the frames clear plastic and cracked. A piece of shiny tape held one of the arms together. In a posh BBC accent she said, "Can you help me find my room? Are you one of the staff? I'm terribly lost though I've been here before. My name is Anne."

It was Anne Szumigalski: a woman the age of my mother, my first breathing, fleshy, *female* poet. I didn't study with her. I was in Ken Mitchell's class. But her presence was palpable. One night, towards the end of what would be many summers at the school, she and I wound up alone, skinny-dipping in Echo Lake across the road, after the sun had set. A group of four or five teenaged boys showed up and plunked down on the beach as we were quietly swimming far from shore. I'm sure they hadn't seen our clothes piled nearby; they didn't know anyone else was there. There was only one way for us to retrieve our garments and leave. As we waded out of the darkness, emerging from the shallow water silvered with moonlight, they jumped to their feet. One gasped, "Where did you come from?"

Anne said with great aplomb, "We're from Planet Poetry," and we picked up our clothes and walked away.

IT IS NIGHT

Wind turns back the sheets of the field.
What needs to sleep, sleeps there.
What needs to rest.

The door has fallen from the moon.
It floats in the slough, all knobs and hinges.

Now the moon's so open
anything could walk right through.

Only the fox is travelling.
One minute he's a cat, the next a coyote.

Enough light to see by
yet my mouth lies in darkness.
What needs to sleep, sleeps there.
What needs to rest.

Outside my mind, the wind is reckoning.
Always there is something
to figure out.

August, 2017

FUZZY WITH MEDICATION, Patrick has moments of cognitive disarray—he forgets what day it is, he has trouble following the plot of an uncomplicated TV show, he doesn't remember if he's taken his morning pills—but I'm grateful his mysterious illness isn't Alzheimer's. One of my friends has had to let her husband go into a care home because he, the most gentle of people, has hit her several times in an explosive rage. He isn't the man she has shared her life with for fifty years. Another friend feels she's lucky that her partner has devolved into a child again. When she leaves the room where she's been reading, he hides her glasses. His antics are charming—except when he forgets where he's stashed them and she needs to drive him for an appointment. She eventually finds them in the bran flakes box, in the cutlery compartment of the dishwasher, in the toe of a rubber boot. At least he's becoming what he once was, a fun-loving, mischievous boy—not someone she no longer feels safe with. But what will happen next?

The steroid called Prednisone that Patrick must swallow to keep his auto-immune disorder from swamping him with pain, inflammation, and an exhaustion so depleting he looks snuffed-out, puts him on edge. He has a word for it and warns me when his irritability spikes—"Watch out. I'm in a predni*zone*." I find it hard not to get cranky too and lash out. I find it hard not to get hurt. Walking on eggshells, yes: eggshells with sharp edges, eggshells made of brittle glass.

Though he's in the house, maybe sitting on the couch beside me, we're not engaging like we used to. It's easy to upset him. As hours go by when we don't talk about anything that matters, I have to remind myself that the man I adore and admire is still there. The man who doesn't snap at me, who is patient, tolerant, kind. The man who works in the garden, who writes, who shops, who cooks, who calls me into our bedroom to make love. Maybe he won't come back, though. Maybe this is the new Patrick with whom I'll spend the rest of our days.

People like to talk about the "new normal," and how the caregiver's task is to get used to it. I pray that this isn't how the time we have left is going to be. But if so, I'll treasure the moments when we do connect, however brief, and expand and redefine what I mean by *love*. This love lacks the physical drive of our early years; we don't flare with passion or anger like we used to in each other's presence. But until his illness, that mellowing-out was okay: ferocity had given way to contentment, explosions to a slow burning we still felt below the surface. It warmed our skin when we sat close, but there was no danger it would conflagrate the rooms we lived in. How far we've travelled from our early years together. And how much we still mean to each other—more, we've said, than ever before.

It's not just the length of our relationship that makes us say that. It's all the things we've done together, even the small, inconsequential ones. It's how we listen when the other speaks, how we seek and give advice, how we hold hands when we're walking down the street, and how my heart jumps when I hear his truck in the driveway, the door opening, and his words, "I'm home."

## LIVING DAY BY DAY

I have no children and he has five,
three of them grown up, two with their mother.
It didn't matter when I was thirty and we met.
*There'll be no children*, he said, the first night
we slept together and I didn't care,
thought we wouldn't last anyway,
those terrible fights,
he and I struggling to be the first
to pack, the first one out the door.
Once I made it to the car before him,
locked him out. He jumped on the hood,
then kicked the headlights in.
Our friends said we'd kill each other
before the year was through.

Now it's decades later.
Neither of us wants to leave.
We are at home with one another,
we are each other's home,
the voice in the doorway,
calling *Come in, come in,*
*it's growing dark.*

Still, I'm often asked if I have children.

Sometimes I answer yes.
Sometimes we have so much
we make another person.
I can feel her in the night
slip between us, tell my dreams
how she spent her day. *Good night*,
she says, *good night, little mother,*
and leaves before I waken.

Across the lawns she dances
in her white, white dress,
her dream hair flying.

Daily I catch sight of the vibrant, confident Patrick, the way you glimpse someone waving from the window of a train pulling out of a station. I wave and wave and long for his return. Then I gather myself, walk the cinder path from the railroad tracks to where I've left the car, pull out of the parking lot and join the stream of traffic because I don't know where to go, what to do.

Several months into Patrick's illness, after leaving him alone at home for the evening, I guided my friends Tina and Patty from our gravel driveway through the side door he'd left unlocked and into our quiet house. The porch light was on but the bedroom was dark. It was around 11:30 p.m. We three had been at a premiere at the Belfry Theatre in downtown Victoria. Patty and Tina live a few hours up island and they were staying overnight. I turned the light on in the spare room and whispered good night, knowing that in our bedroom directly across the hall, Patrick would be asleep, Basho likely curled by his hip, Po Chu hunting moths in the low lights along the garden walk. Through the partly open door, I could hear Patrick's breathing. It hadn't been a good day for him. He'd moved from bed to couch and back to bed again even before I'd left with my friends for the city. Hearing his regular breathing, in and out, in and out, made me relax a little.

The play we'd seen was written by the wife of an Alzheimer's patient. I'd stuffed my pockets with Kleenexes, expecting to weep through the scenes where the main character wrestled with her husband's condition and her mixed feelings about looking after him. That had been part of the advanced publicity surrounding the opening. The tears didn't come. The most engaging parts of the drama revolved around the mother's relationship with her two away-from-home children and the comic exchanges between her and the owner of the retail store where she worked.

In the car on the way home from the theatre, Tina, Patty, and I batted back and forth our reactions to the play. Tina, an actor, a poet and a playwright, was working on a script based on my Mrs. Bentley poems, a series I'd written in the persona of Sinclair Ross's narrator in his novel *As For Me and My House*. Chatting on email and getting together for lunch, she and I were trying to figure out how to electrify dramatic dialogue with the force and rhythms of poetry. How to make the lines sing but still sound unpretentious and colloquial to the audience's ear. We were no Shakespeare—that kind of language didn't come easily.

We'd also talked about the challenge of speaking some kind of inner truth on stage without being messianic or sentimental. For the past year, Tina, Patty, and I had been going to local productions together to learn how others were doing it. It was fun for me to pick apart a play, not out of meanness but out of a desire to understand the form with someone who'd studied in a theatre department, had produced her own work and been on stage. Patty, as a professional musician, knew about performance, too. Did the problems we identified stem from the acting, the directing, or the writing? I loved our analysis—it was like taking a crash course on playwriting. In our discussion of this premiere, the three of us agreed that we wished the writer had gone further with the husband/wife dynamic and the agonies that come with that terrible disease.

Could she not go deeper because he was still alive? We asked this of each other in the darkness of the car as Tina signalled our way out of the city and onto the highway for the thirty-minute drive north on the Saanich Peninsula to Patrick's and my home. Was she protecting him? Was it too painful for her to go there as a writer? Had she been shielding their children from the tough stuff about their mother and father, the less-than-admirable feelings, the anger and blame, the self-pity and denial that accompany sorrow and loss? No one could reproach her for not going where we'd hoped she'd go. Nevertheless, though we'd liked a lot of the play, we felt disappointed.

Maybe that wasn't fair. Every writer knows that words don't come close to what is really happening, especially in times of wrenching grief. There isn't any vocabulary of verity that will touch what it means to live with someone who is disappearing day by day. It would have to be a language of gristle and sinew and broken syntax. It would have to whisper into a chasm of dread and silence. It would have to allow the writer to forgive herself for her need to speak this intimate and private pain.

BECAUSE WE ARE MADE OF MOSTLY WATER

every time we speak
our words are mist, are rain,
clear rivulets chattering

over sand and gravel,
over bones laid deep
in the earth. Sometimes

our words are snow.
Cold alphabets slap the cheeks,
the sting of winter slipping

from your tongue to mine,
and everything inside us
freezes shut. We speak then

as the dead do, all
the rivers knotted with ice,
our mouths odd

with cold and urgently dry
from the effort of making
no sad sound.

What makes a relationship good, so good that thinking of its coming to an end buckles your knees and turns your gut to ice? We have been, I can say without hesitation, devoted. The definition of "devoted" in the Oxford English Dictionary gets away with two fervent adverbs: "*zealously* attached" and "*enthusiastically* loyal or faithful." I buy into both of these, though the former phrase sounds dangerously codependent. One of the most delicious illustrations of devotion comes from Shakespeare's *Othello*: "He hath devoted and given up himself to the contemplation of . . . her parts and graces."

The word is loaded, too, with religious connotations: to devote is "to consecrate." I'm sure Patrick would agree there's been a sacredness to our compact, especially as we've grown older. It's a sacredness that exists outside the walls of a church, though both of us are avid readers of the Bible. One morning he alerts me to the phrase "covenant of salt," which he's discovered appears three times in its pages. We have that covenant, he claims, and goes on to tell me of a Middle Eastern saying that turns two of the commonest ingredients into something blessèd and profound: "There is bread and salt between us." We have cooked a thousand meals for one another, we have held a spoon to the other's mouth and asked if the soup needs more salt, we have broken bread and offered across our table a holy covenant. Day after day after day, we have tasted the brine of each other's skin.

For over half my life, Patrick has been my lover, friend, and partner, everything I'd want a spouse to be, yet during our time together we've resisted the sentimental and the conventionally romantic. Neither of us has wanted to collect or display photographs; we've never owned a camera—though I'm pleased to see, in our publicity shots, we're leaning into each other and laughing. Even now, in his reduced state, he comes up with witticisms as quick as fireflies startling the dark. "At least I can still make you laugh," he says.

We've never lost sound or sight of each other, even when we're in different cities (is that rare or normal for a long relationship?)— yet we forget our anniversary (what year was it we got married?) and neglect to buy flowers on special days; we work alone in our rooms until supper, barely speaking, and we can attend a party at someone else's house and not cross paths until one of us gives the nod that means, "Let's leave."

And then there is our bickering.

Friends who know us well shake their heads. "There they go again," they say, as we spark across a dinner table, vehemently disagreeing with what the other just said. Since we wrote *No Longer Two People* we've mellowed, we've calmed down—but our original feistiness hasn't vanished. Our bantering defines us, it has become a kind of play, a darting in to take a sporty nip then darting out again. The tone of our words may not sound light and harmless, and there's no doubt we easily get annoyed and piss each other off. But the squabbling is part of who we are, and it can't be quashed even when it makes those around us uncomfortable. In *Pursuits of Happiness*, his study of classic Hollywood comedy, Stanley Cavell remarks, "there may be bickering that is itself a mark, not of bliss exactly, but say of caring. As if a willingness for marriage entails a certain willingness for bickering." After an evening where we'd both been particularly pugnacious (do I dare say, Patrick more than me?) I read that passage to him when I came across it after dipping in and out of books on our shelves. Maybe, we agreed with some relief, in spite of the distress of our friends, we were going to be okay.

FIRE BREATHER

When I drank what you gave me I burned
my mouth. So much fire on these lips.
You should have told me.

I was used to tasting your homemade soups
with a wooden spoon, testing the flavour,
the windows steamed so I couldn't see out.

Add more barley, I'd say, or those red spices
from the Nile. You'd save everything, even
tongues, hearts, and pickerel cheeks.

We could be in Japan, our shoes off all the time.
Under my fingers your flesh gives like grass mats,
Blue-Eyed or Brome. Oh, you're a quiet one.

Nothing to show, but inside enough heat
to light the tallow candles you bought
from the butcher who gives you soup bones for free.

After I take you in my mouth I can blow flames
across a room. A strange bed for us to lie in,
all these ashes and my feet still cold.

A willingness for bickering. We certainly have that. We also
have a willingness for touching in public, for holding hands and
sitting close together, me hooking my leg over his, resting my head
on his shoulder, nuzzling my nose just above his collarbone at the
base of his neck and breathing in the smell that is peculiarly him.
Before he shaved his head—there's a code in barber shops, he tells
me; he's been getting a "Number 2: hair is a quarter-inch long"—
I'd lift the curls off the back of his collar and kiss the strawberry
birthmark that few besides him, his mother, and me (and the ex-
lovers I don't want to think about) know is there. Patrick's lower
vertebrae complain if he works too hard outside, my knees creak
and grind when I walk—I had to give up jogging twenty years
ago—but desire has not packed its bag and abandoned us. Less
acrobatic than we used to be, our flesh saggy and worn, we made
love a couple of times a week until he fell ill. Maestro, maestra of

each other's bodies, we relished smelling and touching ai
this familiar yet mysterious being who was him, who was
who cried out and died the little death in each other's ar...s. My
little wolf, he used to call me, my howler monkey.

Have those bodily pleasures been sweeter because of the kind
of friendship we've forged? It offers support and consolation, but
it doesn't let us off the hook. When one of us is being small-
minded or uncharitable, the other intervenes and challenges the
opinion, sometimes gently, sometimes not. I go back to Camus'
*Notebooks, 1951–59*, where I've turned down the page: "If those
whom we begin to love could know us as we were before meeting
them . . . they could perceive what they have made us." We've made
each other better, bigger of heart and mind and spirit. We've also
emboldened the other to speak out, to challenge when it's easier
to be quiet, to honestly express confusion or ignorance about a
topic, to let go and to forgive. I would be a lesser person without
Patrick's tutelage, without his eye on me. And he without mine.

We are separate, solitary selves, independent and opinionated
and unruly. But our love for one another blurs the edges of our *sui
generis* identities. Perhaps it creates a third presence that is not a
shadow but a luminosity that walks beside us, even when we walk
alone. I feel that glow when I go out into my life. Wherever I am,
whatever I meet, whatever I must confront, it gives me courage, it
makes me visible in the strongest sense of my being, knowing I am
adored by someone as extraordinary as my beloved. Does that not
mean I am extraordinary too? Does that not mean I can show,
with all my flaws and insecurities, who I am?

Is it love, then, that makes us what we are? St. Augustine would
answer yes. In the fourth century he wrote, "Such is each as is his
love." I can't help but notice in his short affirmation the double
"is," a minim of the present moment. If that love forsakes today

and dwells only in the past, what will happen to the man or woman who treasured it and then had to let it go? A shadow disappearing is an ominous sign. How much more startling and unsettling if it's the vivid antithesis of a shadow that vanishes from the earth? If one of us falls out of love or—anything is possible—or, if one of us dies, the absence will be greater than the loss of the singular person in bodily form, the singular person with a name. This third presence, this bright being that love gives birth to, will dissipate. And there will be no marked grave, no ashes to scatter, just a lessening that maybe lovers of all ages, in all places, will momentarily feel as it fades out. It will make them shiver.

In Patrick's convocation address at the University of British Columbia in 2013, he refers to the wise people he has read. He says the one thing they abide with is governed by "a good and honest love." Can I say that's the kind we have? I must ask him. We've shared, too, in every sinew of our being a love for the natural world and a deep sadness for what our species is doing to the multitude of life forms it deems less important than itself. In every house we've lived in, Patrick and I have made a garden. And he has been the master of that husbandry.

Patrick writes in his memoir: "Every stone in my garden is a story, every tree a poem. I barely know myself in spite of the admonishments of wise men and women who tell me I must know my life in order to live it fully. What I know is that I live in this place where words are made. What we are is a garden. I believe that." His words and mine have been inspired and nurtured by the soil we tend, whether we write of joy or sorrow, of spring arriving or winter never letting go. This is where we come together, in our garden, our bodies, our poems; our beginning and our end are in these places.

Our hours of working outside, singly or side by side, have been a way to express contrition to the earth, to nurture habitats that attract bees and dragonflies, birds, beetles, and spiders, that shelter fish and turtles, raccoons, bats, mice, and moles. Our sweat and muscle strain become part of the soil we dig and weed and fertilize and part of the water we tend so the fish can slip through our dreams. At our first pond in Saskatoon in the mid-1980s, as we sat outside at dusk watching the koi rising to the touch of Patrick's fingers, as he had trained them to do, he said, "The fish are the water's thoughts." A man who can come up with that is a man I'll never leave, I said to myself. It was over thirty years ago. In caring for our patch of earth, we make a home for each other, we become each other's home, no matter how often we've had to move for residencies, for part-time jobs, for sessional appointments, and finally for my position at the University of Victoria. Where we go, we go together, and what we've left behind, both inside and out, has been made more beautiful through our love and labour.

## A GOOD DAY TO START A JOURNAL

The only way to tell you is to write
this down, our lives a journal
with notes about the weather, perhaps
a grocery list and appointments never kept
because the sparrows sing for seeds
in our apple tree, and the spider
at the centre of her web demands
your poet's eye to hold her still.

From the window I watch you digging
in one of the sweaters you'll wear
till the wool is worn thin and I insist
on putting it away. I save each one

as if your mother who knitted them
wanted what little warmth is left
to make something smaller, a sweater
for the boy who curled inside her belly
as she waited in the spring for the pale
buds of fingers to unfurl and bloom.

Earlier in bed your hands cold from the soil,
I wept after I cried out, not knowing why.
All these years together and some days
there's such pleasure in our bodies
as they move through the seasons, far
from the beauty they were born to. Now
they shine like parchment, worn by fingers
by the spittle on the thumb as we turn
a page. We read each other nearsightedly,
hands and tongues and even toes find where
the skin gives way. Since I cannot say
it right, for you today I must try

to keep this journal. Write:
March 26, and a little cold.
Write: Overnight the plum tree
has become one blossom. Write:
The days are getting longer
because my lover in the garden
turns and turns the earth.

In a chapter dedicated to our garden, the editors and writers
of the book *Beauty by Design*, Rosemary Bates and Bill Terry, sum-
marize our different sensibilities. Their statement is about our

response to horticulture, but it applies as neatly to our relationship: "Their gardening perspectives are different, yet oddly compatible." Oh, yes, I say, revisiting the passage six years after the book came out, especially enjoying their use of the word *oddly*. They go on to quote Patrick, his words explaining better than anything our opposite yet complementary perspectives. How lucky we are to have found each other, to have found this small postlapsarian paradise far from both of our childhood landscapes.

I was extremely nearsighted as a child, almost blind, everything almost a complete blur. I had to imagine much of the world surrounding me, but I had no idea what was there. What I did see was everything very, very close up. I spent my time walking with my head down and I still do that. I'd look at what was right in front of my feet because I didn't want to trip and fall.

On the other hand, Lorna sees everything, because she grew up on the prairie, where there are no impediments. For her, everything is vast distance and horizon. Here, she'd trip over a pebble because she's not looking at where she's walking. But then, there's nothing to trip over on the prairie. I grew up in a valley; Lorna grew up on a continent.

So, we're perfectly suited to one another. I'll say, "Look at that tiny beetle by the stone." And Lorna will say, "Isn't that fascinating, but look at those geese flying overhead." I won't have noticed them. We see these two worlds together all the time, and it's the same in the garden.

Reading this passage again this morning, Patrick so wrecked he went back to bed after his first cup of coffee, I shiver with fear over what the future will bring.

Who am I if not my beloved's? What will I see?

April, 2018

OUT OF THE hospital for a few months (are our lives getting back to normal?) but still on a lot of medication, Patrick hasn't built back his strength but he's getting there. I'm booked for several events at the Edmonton Poetry Festival, including the keynote address, a reading, and a workshop. It will boost this year's income, reduced substantially since Patrick had to cancel his private teaching. He's been unable to muster the concentration he needs to prepare for and facilitate such demanding sessions. I've squeezed in three extra days in the city before the poetry festival to work with Tina, along with four actors, a movement coach, and a dramaturge committed to getting the Mrs. Bentley poems into a script that will come alive on stage. Before I flew out for Edmonton in the late afternoon, Patrick had been building a fence. He can work for thirty minutes or so and then he has to stop, but at least he isn't spending most of the day in bed.

By lunchtime, he'd dug two holes with an auger, resting in between. Normally he liked to work on his own, but I went out to help, and he was happy to see me. I spilled water from the hose over the dry cement in the wheelbarrow while he stirred with a shovel. Then I held the first post as he tipped the barrow and poured in the sludge. "You look sexy in your carpenter's leather apron," I teased, the pouch at the side full of nails, the hammer and measuring tape hooked on a loop. "You better have that on when I get home."

Though the cherry trees thicken with pink blossoms in our front yard, from my hotel room in Edmonton I can see skiffs of snow in the shady creases along the North Saskatchewan River, and the cloudless blue sky crackles with cold. I send Patrick a message around six a.m. Pacific time. No response. Maybe he's slept in or he's at the fence already. I head out for a brisk hour-long walk along the riverbank, then back in my room, after finding nothing from him, I send another text: "Where are you? I'm getting worried." No response. And he doesn't answer his cell phone. I call our home number. Someone picks up the receiver. "Hello, hello—Is that you, Patrick? Are you okay?" There's no voice on the other end of the line. A muffled silence, a breath?

I phone the wife of Patrick's brother John because John doesn't always answer his calls. They live in a townhouse complex about fifteen minutes away. I get her voice mail. "Claudine, it's Lorna. I'm probably just being silly but I'm worried about Patrick. Please get in touch when you hear this."

In twenty minutes, she calls back. She was at the grocery store. I ask her to drive to the house and if he doesn't answer the door, to walk in. "I'm sure he's fine, but just in case," I say.

An hour later my cell phone rings. "He's on the couch," she says. "He doesn't want to talk to you."

"I don't understand."

"He says he's incapable of talking to you."

"Is he sick? What's going on?"

She doesn't know what to do. She's going to get John and bring him back to our house. They have only one car so she'll drive to their townhouse, and then he'll drive back. When she phones me again an hour later, it's to say that John has called an ambulance. "Patrick's in emergency," she says, "and we're sitting in the waiting room until we can talk to a doctor. We'll let you know when we find out anything."

Something isn't making sense. Yesterday, before I flew out, he was cutting lumber and pounding boards. He's never happier than when he's building something. Now he's in the hospital? I catch a cab from my hotel to the theatre department at the University of Alberta—they've given us a rehearsal space—and meet the actors who've been working with Tina and the dramaturge on my poems for the past few days. They're anxious to show me what they've done. "I have to leave my phone on," I tell them. "There's an emergency at home." I try to concentrate on their performance, offering advice, words of praise, suggestions. Finally the phone rings.

Claudine explains that Patrick was unable to give his name or birthdate to the paramedics when they got to the house. His whole body shook, he'd lost control of his bowels, he was unconscious when they came through our door. I ask Claudine to get the emergency room doctor to contact me and I call the director of the poetry festival to explain I'm going to have to cancel my events over the next three days and book the soonest flight home. I return to the rehearsal room to watch a scene between two actors pretending to be a husband and wife playing a game of crib. Then they show me a re-enactment of one of my poems that ends, "For the first time I can imagine life without him." I have to leave the room.

In the hall, I lean into the tall window and press my forehead against the glass. Snow is just beginning to fall, the flakes so large and dry and well-defined they could have been cut from blank paper by children in a one-room school. This of course is not Edmonton's first snowfall of the season and may not be its last, but for me it feels like the first, since I arrived in this northern city only a day ago. The sky-born crystals that seem not to want to touch the ground take me back to my childhood, the joy of pulling on my boots and jacket, dashing through the porch to the yard and wading through an immaculate accumulation of stars, my tracks the only sign of a living earthly presence plotting my journey from the house to the alley. Now, waiting for the phone to ring, I'm tempted to flee outside away from the actors and from what is going on at home, to stand alone in that soft, white falling that stops and hushes almost everything.

### THE HOUR OF SNOW

Everything quiets, everything
moves hesitant and slow, even
the feisty pup flops down, his head
between his paws, and in his dream
there's no running after anything.

Outside, the fields pull cold and brightness
over them, those wind-washed sheets.
Time to consider snow's sophistry,
its mortar and mend,
before fields resume their job,
laying down the path to heaven.

You walk into your breath—small
frosted cloud in front of you—
and breathe it in,

brief memento of who you were
a heartbeat past. Snow gives you
this hour to say goodbye to everything,
your hair, the thick and thin of it,
gone white with grief.


Sixteen hours after I started calling home from my hotel in Edmonton, Patrick's brother picks me up at the Sidney airport. It's 10:30 at night. John tells me Patrick's in our small local hospital, not the large health centre in Victoria where he'd been a patient three months ago. Those found in deep crisis and rescued by ambulance crews are always rushed to the closest care facility, John explains. Patrick has been there since the morning, hooked up to antibiotics and water; he'd fallen into toxic shock and no one knew why. John continues, "There's a bit of a mess waiting for you at home."

He turns onto our country road that has no streetlamps and pulls up to our house, the windows dark. I slide out of the car, grab my bag from the back seat, and he drives away. I stand in the driveway for a moment, watching his tail lights disappear, mustering the strength to enter the empty rooms where earlier in the day strangers rushed in with a stretcher and carried my beloved away. The house looks small and hunched, as if it has closed in on itself, holding some kind of inner unspeakable pain.

The smell hits me as soon as I walk through the door. On the couch in the living room Patrick's soiled pajama bottoms and bathrobe are heaped in a pile. I hold my breath, bundle up the clothing, rush it down the hall and throw it in the washing machine. Then I check out the bathroom. John told me there was a mess there too. Scat on the floor, the toilet seat, on the top of the electric heater. I can't imagine the explosion, the breakdown of Patrick's body. Before I drive to the hospital, I scrub the bathroom and the couch with the strongest cleaning fluid I can find, I feed the cats, stuff Patrick's night kit with what I think he'll need, and search for his hearing aids. They're nowhere to be found. And what about his cell phone?

Oh, no. Was it in the pocket of his bathrobe? His hearing aids too? Are they in the wash? The door of our front-loading machine locks and won't open once it starts filling with water. I think I hear a clunking among the soft clothing but there's nothing I can do except turn off the machine. I'll take care of it later.

Fifteen minutes after being dropped off at our house, I'm in my car and speeding to the small hospital about ten miles away. I'm beating myself up for wasting that time cleaning up: why did I delay? Am I so scared to see him? The main door is locked, the foyer dark, but John told me there's a way to get to the ward through the emergency entrance, and there's a phone on the wall where a recorded voice will give the patients' room numbers. It works— "Patrick Lane," I say; the mechanical voice replies, "Room 425-D."

The vacant corridor is dim with night lights. What a peaceful place the hallways are in the witching hours. No visitors, no meal trolleys rattling on the hard floors, no janitors with their wheeled buckets and mops, no gaggle of visitors bearing balloons or flowers, no one weeping. Anything loud, anything dramatic is going on out of sight or is waiting for the morning. In the silence of the corridor, I will myself to move, to find his room, to face whatever condition he is in. I can't put it off any longer.

Room 425. Four beds labelled A, B, C, D. Patrick is in the farthest, with the curtains pulled. I step through as if onto a stage designed for the sick. Bags and tubes and monitors. Lit-up numbers and a green line peaking and falling on the small screen, the beating of my loved one's heart. The single window looks out on the dark. On the blue pillowcase, his dear face, the fine strands of hair on his forehead wet with sweat. His skin looks flushed. He is sleeping, his breathing deep and steady—oh, how many times I've listened to his nightly breathing—he doesn't know I am here. I kiss his cheek, his eyelids, his stubbled chin, sit on the edge of the bed and let the tears come. It has been a long, long day.

On the side table, his hearing aids, the size and shape of kidney beans, buzz as if they've noticed my presence. They make a high electronic squeal when they've been removed from the ears and left close together, a reminder to the owner to disconnect the batteries so they don't wear out. At least they aren't turning around and around in the wash, listening attentively to their own demise. I separate them, then glance around the bed. I don't see a cell phone. I check the drawers but nothing's there. That means his phone is soaking in a pool of soapy water on the bottom of the locked washing machine.

At the acute care station in the ward the night nurse, a young woman with waist-length red hair like our oldest granddaughter, confirms what I already know: my husband was unconscious when they loaded him on the stretcher. He didn't know his name. "A complete breakdown," she says, "toxic shock, but now he's in good hands. He's on a dose of super-antibiotics. His heart, blood pressure, oxygen are being monitored."

"Have you talked to him?" I ask. "Since they brought him in? Did he gain consciousness?"

"Yes, he was even able to joke. He's quite the guy."

"Is he in danger now?" I dare to ask, "Is he going to die?"

"He's good tonight," she says. "You look beat, go home, you can talk to the doctor tomorrow."

I retrace my steps down the night-hushed hallway to the front doors and walk out to the visitors' parking lot. My car's the only one there, though a black truck pulls up in front of emergency and a young man hobbles out of the passenger side, his foot wrapped in a bloody towel. "Fuck off," he shouts to whoever's driving. In the light cast from his open door, I catch a glimpse of a woman through the windshield. Her blond hair spills from a red ball cap, her round face twists into an angry grimace. She reaches across the narrow seat and slams the door. Tall behind the steering wheel of the big truck, she looks as if she could plow her way through snow and mud, through whatever lies ahead and keep on going. She guns the motor and pulls away. I want to run beside her, yank open the door and hop in. "Take me where you're going. Show me how to do it. How to be so tough."

When I get home, I feed the cats, pour myself a wine, and pick up Patrick's latest book of poems to find some solace in his words when I can't talk to him or he to me. The pages fall open at "Bokuseki." The lines seem an emblem for this difficult start of spring. I pray they are not prophetic. *Iris blades cut through the last ice on the pond. / Emblems of endurance, they are what a man knows / who asks of the grey clouds they witness his passing.*

April, 2018

BECAUSE PATRICK'S MEDICAL TEAM in our small hospital can't figure out the cause of his fever, after a week in the acute care ward, housed with four other patients, he's put into an isolation room where the air and its stowaway germs can't circulate. Anyone who enters, including the nurses, has to don a long-sleeved gown tied in the back, an over-the-nose-and-mouth mask that smells of chemicals, and blue latex gloves. Does this cover-up protocol make the nurses slow to respond when he presses the call button? He has to press it often because the intravenous tubes dripping high-powered antibiotics into his veins continue to block and the machine incessantly beeps, the electronic noise growing louder and more unnerving minute by minute, the intervals between the warning signals shorter, until someone fixes the problem.

A couple of days ago, the mind-piercing screech needled into his brain for forty-five minutes. An email he sent from his iPad pleaded with me to phone the nursing station to get someone to take action. I dialed the number; no one picked up. I hopped in the car, sped down the road to the hospital and rushed into his room without covering up. The morning nurse had finally responded and adjusted the intravenous machine. I reprimanded her when she came back in to take his temperature. "He could have fallen," I said, "and lain helpless on the floor for almost an hour." In this isolation chamber, the door to the hall leads to a small anteroom with a sink where you wash your hands before and after; then there's another door that opens to the space with the bed. Because any cries from the patient can't be heard, Patrick is completely dependent on the staff responding to his finger on the red button. It is gut-wrenching to see him so helpless.

They are testing for every bug and virus, including TB. The prophylactics are to protect others from him but also to protect him from germs outsiders might bring in. When any kind of infection slips into his system, he crashes into toxic shock. Even the common cold is highly dangerous. That explains the room's antiseptic dullness, I guess. It is as sterile as it gets—nothing extra, everything spare—microbes have few places to thrive. Beyond the medical paraphernalia, there is nothing to look at, including outside the window where the earth has been dug up for some kind of construction. It looks like a mass grave. I can't think of that.


When my father was dying, the only thing without function in his room in the Swift Current hospital was a photograph of the chestnut head of a horse on the wall above his bed. The horse wasn't looking straight on but over its left shoulder so that the long, thick neck was prominent. It radiated health and power in a room where countless people had relinquished both. During my mother's and my vigil, I stared at the picture, thinking it carried a message but not knowing what it might be. Was it there to remind me of my father's love of his family's racehorse, Tony, and the adventure they had shared when he was a boy?

Tony, an inauspicious-looking grey gelding, won all the races, at least that's what my father claimed, at sports days around Success, the town closest to the Crozier farm. The stakes were so high that the animals were in danger of being messed with in their stalls. Someone once pierced Tony's leg with a stiff hair, my father said. It made him lame enough to be taken out of the running the entire day.

For one of the biggest races, to avoid the chance of injury or meddling of any kind, my dad's father asked him to ride Tony at night through the Sandhills to reach the track clandestinely and register him the next morning just before the event was called. I guess that kind of last-minute entry was possible then. If this all worked out, Dad would get to race him. Just a kid, around twelve years old, he was the right size for a jockey. And he had the right temperament for a covert nightly journey. In other words, he was sneaky.

When Patrick first met my father the year I was the writer-in-residence at the community college in Swift Current, he asked Dad to help him find a second-hand car. We were renting a small house across from my parents' and we saw a lot of them. At various family meals, Patrick had listened to my father brag about how he could strike a bargain and get the best of anyone. "He could even trick the devil," my mother said.

A couple of days after Patrick's request, my father pulled up to the curb in front of our place in an old beater we'd never seen before. "This'll cost you 400 bucks," he told Patrick. "A deal." He said he'd met a guy at the Legion. The next morning my mom marched across the street, knocked on our door, and when Patrick answered, handed him $200. My father had charged twice what he'd really paid, and she'd shamed him into giving her the money. Patrick was outraged.

"You don't do this to family," he said to me after Mom had left.

"That's just my father," I replied. "You can't take it personally."

When you hit the Sandhills in southwest Saskatchewan, you'd swear you were in the Sahara. This is a countryside flensed: there is only sand and a fleshless pelt of sky pegged to the corners of two thousand square miles of dunes the colour of coyotes, of antelopes, of prairie dogs. I try to picture that boy and horse alone at night, above them the sky riddled with constellations. The cross-country journey they had to undertake wasn't that far, around fifty miles or so, and my father rode slowly, navigating by the stars like a Bedouin. That simile is not my father's. He'd have said he followed the Big Dipper and was scared of getting lost.

Even had it been daylight, there were no trees or stone cairns to punctuate the monochromatic terrain, and to make it worse, the ground itself wouldn't stay still. Wind, every hour, every season, had its way, shaping and reshaping the mounds and rills and long, flat reaches, burying the stunted shrubs and resurrecting them, rubbing the fine particles, one against the other, so the only sound was a gritty, pre-verbal hissing that filled your head. Though their trek through these uninhabited barrens lasted just a few hours, it was one of the most thrilling things my father would ever do. His father had chosen him instead of his younger brother and would be waiting for him as morning broke at the track.

Though the horse in the hospital photograph was a different colour, a different breed, was it Tony watching over him during his final days? Would he take my father's worn-out body that weighed no more than a boy's and carry him through the dark of the desert, the ground undulating, dunes rising and sinking like waves, wind blowing sand into the tracks so no one could follow or know where they were going, so no one would know they'd been there—his breath, the horse's breath, the creak of saddle leather, the soft sift under the hooves and against the boy's skin and the gelding's hide, the only sounds in this midnight journey to the other world?

Laura, a friend from Michigan who's taken several classes with me over the last ten years at Wintergreen Studios outside of Kingston, is the living embodiment of what I've been teaching for years—that writing can be a consolation, that a poet needs to go to the dark places and open a crack for the feeblest of light, even if that glimmer doesn't slip into the heart for years after the words appear on the page. Sometimes the light of your own poems never makes its way inside you, never gives you hope, but it's possible others will find it, that it will bring them some kind of sustenance, some modicum of comfort. Does that matter to the writer? I don't know. When I am at my lowest, not knowing how to find my way through the days of worry and fear, Laura writes, "Sometimes poems are just poems." It's strangely comforting.

Two weeks before my regular teaching stint at Wintergreen was about to begin in May of 2017, Laura's twenty-six-year-old daughter killed herself in the apartment she'd rented in another city. Among her daughter's papers, Laura found a list of guns—and along with that, a receipt for a Smith & Wesson. It was the weapon the young woman had used to shoot herself. Hers was a family not used to guns. How had she even known what to buy?

In the depths of shock and grief, Laura showed up at my workshop to write poetry. Together with my friend Rena, who was the director of the retreat centre, I had told her she'd be welcome if that was where she needed to be. She wanted to articulate, even in gasps and stutters, her unsayable anguish—for herself, but also for a reader. She wanted to discover what was hers to tell and what should remain the untold part of her daughter's story.

The deal Laura and I agreed upon before she arrived was that I'd treat her poems as works of art, not therapy, that I'd critique them and help her make them the best they could be. I have learned how to do that in my life with another writer. To set aside the harrowing emotions that generate the tropes and images, and go back to the words themselves, the nouns and verbs and adjectives laid one by one across the page.

A SUMMER'S SINGING

Where does that singing start, you know,
that thin sound—almost pure light?
Not the birds at false dawn or their song
when morning comes, feathered throats
warm with meaning. A different kind of music.

Listen, it is somewhere near you.
In the heart, emptied of fear,
stubbornly in love
with itself at last, the old
desires a ruined chorus,
a radiant, bloody choir.

Where does the singing start?
Here, where you are, there's room

between your heartbeats,
as if everything you have ever been
begins, inside, to sing.


Directly across the road from our driveway is Coles Bay park. Close to nine acres, it's a stand of trees growing on two sides of a deep ravine that drops about twenty feet to the ocean. The trees are second- or third-growth cedars and firs and Garry oak along with younger maples, all of them shrouded in English ivy, an invasive plant some idiot settler brought from the Old Country a century ago and let loose in the wild. Carpeting most of the forest floor, it's impossible to eradicate, but before he fell ill, Patrick headed out with secateurs twice a week to cut through the vines and free the trees from choking. I started to go with him. It was three years of hard, dirty work; when we hacked through a stem then yanked at the ivy that towered above, all kinds of debris— insects, dust, chunks of bark, twigs, needles, and sticky sap—fell on our heads. Some of the vines were as thick as a linebacker's thigh and Patrick had to use a bow saw to slice through their grip. I found it difficult to keep my footing. Logs I thought would hold me turned out to be punky and collapsed with my weight. Countless times I slammed onto my bum into a well of deep, wet foliage and had to grab a root to pull myself upright. We both laughed at my clumsiness. This was one way to learn the secrets of trees.

Patrick, who unlike me is used to forests, is more graceful, but once, out there alone and balancing on the edge of the ravine to get to the other side of a large fir, his foot broke through the downed trunk that had been supporting him and he tumbled vertically through fifteen feet of blackberry canes, salal, and fallen, multi-pronged branches to finally bang his body into the stones at the bottom where the creek ran into the bay. I heard him come through the door and rose from my office chair to find a wounded, bleeding man. His face and arms were scraped and scored, and he'd cracked his ribs on his right side, which hit the ground first. Yet after just a week away from it, we went back for two more years of cutting ivy until every tree in the grove was freed from its green strangulation.

There's probably no better way to get to know a forest. We touched each one of the four hundred or so trees, and they touched us back. No words were needed, but we *felt* each other, across species boundaries, across the years, across their knowing and ours, bark and flesh, sap and blood, speaking and not speaking. We shared the same wind and rain during our hours among them. We suffered through drought. Perhaps it was fancy, but I felt sure the cedars and firs, some of them hundreds of years old, freed from decades of choking, breathed a sigh of relief and stretched their limbs higher into the sky. We had helped them do that. Had we ever done anything better?

Through our bedroom's sliding glass doors, from my pillow I can look across the front yard and the road to the tall outer fringe of green that borders the park. Each of the trees has felt our hands, heard our voices and breathed in our smell as we've torn at the ivy. Not knowing what to pray to during Patrick's first hospital stay, when I feared he wasn't getting better, every night I prayed to them—to the cedars, the firs, the oaks, the scrub maples. He was so good to you, I said out loud. Please use all of your ancient energy, your primal power to bring this man who worked so hard to save you safely home. May he, like you, reach tall and strong, his beautiful, day-dreamy head touching the sky. May he grow older than old beside you.

From THOREAU SAID A WALK CHANGES THE WALKER

There are weeks in the forest
when your whole body is
a word even you can't utter
but the trees, in their
deep listening,
hear.

Early May, 2018

WHEN I HUG Patrick goodbye after they deliver his supper, I feel emptied out like a dried seed-pod that rattles if you shake it. Basho is waiting in the carport as I drive in. I'm sure he no longer hears the car—I can't figure out what alerts him to my arrival. Is it the time of day, something he can still intuit through the changing of the light? Maybe a coolness as the sun sinks below the trees and the evening breeze lifts his fine hair? I arrive home on schedule around 6:30, in time to make something for myself for supper, have a glass of wine, and feed the cats. I can't get in touch with Patrick until I buy him a new cell phone—indeed, I did throw the old one in the wash—and in some ways the imposed silence is a release. It's just me and the cats and dozens of messages on the answering machine and on my email asking about him. Sometimes I can talk to friends, sometimes I can't. Most people tell me how strong I'm being, but really they don't have a clue. They can't see me when I'm alone; they can't hear me when I'm off the phone, setting the table for one.

NO MUSIC IN IT

The sun takes longer to rise:
it bears a burden it cannot carry.
Darkness lengthens in the day
and inside me
until I walk on stilts of it,
looking down on everything.

I take no pleasure. After dawn
a raven passes overhead.
He takes none either. Measures
daylight's this and this
on noisy wings. Blowing in
a bone flute that has no holes.

Before Patrick was moved into isolation, he shared a room with
four men, all of them older, all of them in some kind of acute care.
Two slept most of the time, but the third one, who never left his
bed, stayed awake and talked to himself. He fell quiet, perversely
so, only when two older women, who I assumed were his daughters, sat by his bed in the late afternoons and helped him with his
dinner. They asked him questions he didn't answer: he looked at
one then the other, cocking his head like a robin eavesdropping on
worms; he opened his mouth when they lifted a spoon to his lips;
he didn't make a sound. As soon as they left, he started vocalizing
again, his voice soft but persistent. I was amazed by his syntax,
the elegance of his style, though I had to work hard to prevent
his constant stream of queries from driving me mad. What had
he done in his younger life? I wondered. Had he been a teacher,
a lawyer, a minister? Here he was merely an old man in a bed,

dependent on the kindness of his daughters and strangers with stethoscopes, needles, and trays, the kindness of someone who may or may not answer his calls.

*Will someone help me?*
*Why is the light switch in your room?*
*Is there a venue for me today?*
*Will she help me?*
*Am I supposed to help you?*
*The windows are wrong.*
*Will I get anything to eat?*
*Am I doing anything in consideration of you or with you?*
*What am I doing tomorrow? Excuse me, I mean today.*
*Will someone tell me the time?*
*Will you help me get a wash?*
*Where do I go from here?*
*Have I been sick?*
*Is there anyone to help me?*

During the first couple of months of our living together in Winnipeg, I discovered in myself an incredible power to destroy, to zap another person with a bolt of bad intention. How I wish now I could summon that inner force to heal, not wound, to enter Patrick's body and annihilate the cells that are out of whack.

That fall, in his role as writer-in-residence at the University of Manitoba, Patrick invited two poets from B.C. whom he'd mentored; I'll call them Rick and Cathy. They were both around my age, maybe a little older. Patrick had set up a reading for them, booked a room on campus, hung up posters, and invited all the Winnipeg writers we'd met. He'd buy the beer. He was hoping to forge a link between the new generation of prairie poets and those on the coast. That was part of his generosity and his belief that poetry should be a fellowship. We should all support one another.

Patrick's two friends would be our first overnight guests at the house we were renting in the city's north end. It was a classy place, built for the metropolitan of the biggest Ukrainian church in the city. After he died, one of his acolytes bought it, walling off a third of the main floor for his own living quarters but keeping the rest the way it had been, as a kind of amateur museum. The rooms included the religious leader's furniture—even the big oak desk where he'd composed his homilies and a large aquarium full of fish, mainly neons and goldfish. Two snails the size of fat plums crawled up the glass walls, grazing on algae, and crawled down again. The tank glowed with its own uncanny light by the red, flocked sofa.

We'd first arrived at this address, which I'd circled in the "Rooms for Rent" section of the paper, with a sense of unease—the number of rooms had been listed, and the fact that it was furnished and boasted its own entrance, but there'd been no mention of the cost. When I phoned to ask, the man who answered and who identified himself as the landlord wouldn't tell me. "Come and see it," he said. We'd found that odd.

A balding, middle-aged man in his early fifties, about a decade older than Patrick but dressed like my grandfather in his going-to-town clothes—brown pants with a belt and a tan work shirt, tucked in—had answered our knock at the door and led us into the foyer. He introduced himself as Howard and, like a guide at a historical site, regaled us with the house's pedigree. He was particularly proud of the desk where the metropolitan had spent so many hours turning his wisdom into words. "What do you think this suite is worth?" he asked. He had a slight accent that I thought must be Ukrainian. We were in that part of town and he worshipped the religious leader as only a true follower, born of the same culture, would. "Before you answer, I'll walk you through," he said.

After checking out the hardwood floors and scatter rugs, the leather wainscotting in the study that doubled as a dining room, the long formal table and matching chairs, not to mention the oak desk and the aquarium, we told him with regret that it was worth more than we could afford. For the three weeks since our arrival in town, we'd been living in a dump of an apartment in a four-storey brick building close to the downtown. Only one burner on the stove worked, the toilet leaked, the closet doors had been ripped off by a previous tenant. The rent was $250 a month, about all we could manage. With his monthly child-support payments, Patrick's stipend and my grant were barely enough to get us through the year, and we hoped to stretch our income for longer than that if nothing came up the next fall. We didn't know it then, but this would be our survival pattern over the next fifteen years.

What did we do for a living, Howard wanted to know. "We're poets," I said, "and Patrick's here for an eight-month stint at the university."

"How much can you pay?"

There was an awkward pause. "Three hundred dollars," Patrick said. That was less than half of what Howard could ask for.

"It's yours."

Our future landlord, it turned out, had a deep affection for poetry, the kind that came from someone who'd fled an oppressive country where it was poets who told the truth, he said, and in doing so, put their lives on the line. In the Ukraine, he and a couple of friends had risked their freedom to produce pages of verse by writers in exile, including the Polish poet Czeslaw Milosz. He remembered mimeographing one of Milosz's small books late at night. When he and his fellow clandestine printers opened the door at three a.m., they walked out into a lineup of people who'd heard about what they were doing and were anxious to hold a copy in their hands. The books were gone before the boxes could be carried to the van waiting in the street. What he revered as much as the metropolitan, he told us, was books. When alive, his religious leader would have welcomed two writers, Howard said, especially two poor ones like us. He could tell by looking that we were the real thing. There were few times in our lives that poetry would bring us out-of-the-blue financial benefits. This was one of them.

Before Patrick went to pick up his friends at the airport, he confessed that he'd slept with Cathy. The last time had been a few months ago, just before he left B.C. for Saskatchewan to find me and start our crazy journey together. Because he'd given everything he had, including all the money from the sale of his house, to his wife and kids, he borrowed $100 from Cathy for gas. She and her husband were rich; he didn't think he'd have to pay it back. "Maybe that makes me a whore," he said. On his way to me, he hadn't even splurged for a motel, but had slept crunched in the back seat of his car pulled off the highway when he was too sleepy to drive any further, and he'd washed and shaved in gas-station bathrooms. "It meant nothing," he said, "to her or me, but I thought you should know." Okay, I thought. I can handle that. I wasn't an innocent—I'd had my peccadillos too. He went on to say, "She's still married, but she and Rick have got a thing going. I think you'll like them."

Although I swore that I'd try to like her, I was pleased to see that Cathy, a short woman with a pretty face, was chubby, and the pale blond hair that grazed her shoulders looked as dry as wheat stubble in a fallow field. Too many years of bleach and blow drying? I felt guilty noting things like that, but I couldn't stop myself. Rick was gangly and awkward and, in spite of his long legs, slow-moving. He hunched when he walked, as if he carried a sack on his back and he didn't know where he wanted to go. He made his living working in a print shop in Kelowna and this was his first invitation to a reading outside of that city. It was a big deal for both of them.

Considering the fierceness I felt for Patrick in our early months, Cathy probably didn't stand a chance, but during the first day of their visit, she did three things that infuriated me. The first had to do with poetry: she metaphorically patted me on the head because she'd published two real books and my first collection was just a chapbook. Her press was an established house in B.C.; mine a new one in Saskatoon. She'd never heard of Thistledown, she said. Then she came face to face with my childhood landscape. We'd taken them for a drive past the city limits so they could see the long golden reach of the prairies undulating all the way to the horizon, clouds building in inky blue layers overhead, the last of the sun breaking through like the mind of a god the first morning of creation. That's how I would have described it, but I kept quiet. I wanted to hear their praise for this beautiful rolling land. "What do people *do* here?" she asked. "It's so boring. There's nothing but emptiness."

Back at the house, Rick and Patrick took off to play pool. They couldn't get out fast enough. Glad to escape the tension, I assumed. I went for a run along the river beneath the big Manitoba maple trees, lecturing myself with each exhalation to act like a grown-up, to be nice. The sky up ahead was noisy with geese coming down from the huge marshes north of town on the first stretch of their long journey south. The light that danced on the leaves had been strained through honey, a hint of the autumnal gold to come. When I got back, I had a shower; Cathy was napping in the room she was sharing with Rick. I got dressed, poured some wine, and started to make dinner. After an hour or so, I heard the men come into the house, laughing. "Hey, Cathy," Rick said, "I beat him."

In a red Chinese robe, Cathy drifted into the kitchen, where I was slicing onions for a stew and keeping my eye on the biscuit dough rising under a cloth in a big bowl. "You should have known this wasn't going to be easy, you know," she said. "After all, Patrick and I have been lovers for years and we still care for one another. You've just entered the picture. How long's it been? A few weeks?"

"Stay here," I told Cathy. I put down my knife, my eyes stinging from the onions, and marched into the living room. "Patrick," I said, "come with me." Back in front of the stove where the pots were simmering, I said, "Cathy just told me you were lovers and had been for years. You told me it was nothing—you slept with her two or three times. Who's telling the truth here?"

Patrick said, "C'mon, Cathy. You know it was just a casual thing for both of us." He looked at me. "It wasn't more than what I said."

"Leave the kitchen now," I said to both of them. "I'm making dinner."

After an uncomfortable meal at the metropolitan's big oak dining room table, a repast made tolerable by bottles of wine, Patrick took Cathy for a walk. When they came back an hour later, two Winnipeg poets, George Amabile and George Morrissette, had joined Rick and me with a case of beer. Patrick had invited them to meet his friends. Cathy settled in the armchair in front of the aquarium directly across the room from me. Patrick sat beside me. He whispered, "I think I sorted things out. For one thing, I told her not to treat you so badly. You're my woman and that's the way it's gonna be."

Cathy interrupted the back-and-forth banter of the four men in the room. They were arguing about the Black Mountain school, whether it had harmed Canadian poetry or done it good. It wasn't

Charles Olson who was at fault, Patrick insisted, it was his imitators. I was just listening. I'd never heard of Black Mountain before. "There's something I want to say," Cathy said. I was overreacting to the situation, she said, but she wanted to be friends, she thought we could be friends.

Something dark and spiked with bile spun in the pit of my stomach. Raw, primal, loud with rage, but nothing anyone could hear. Rick must have felt it—he lifted his feet off the floor. Cathy looked at me, waiting for my reply. George Amabile said, "Holy shit." I said nothing, but if a cartoonist had been there, he'd have drawn lightning bolts zapping from my eyes at the woman across the room. If spit had hit my skin, it would have sizzled. The other George said, "Yikes," and lifted his feet too. Cathy didn't explode or turn to smoke. Silent, she sunk lower in her chair, as if a dark, invisible undertow was pulling on her ankles. I had wanted more.

The force of my rage, aimed so fiercely at its target, dissipated quickly. In its aftermath, I don't remember anyone speaking about what had happened. I couldn't find words for it. What I had done had emptied me of energy and, for the time being, malice. I could feel it leave my body like air leaving a leaking balloon. Had I really turned into some kind of nasty wonder woman with the power to destroy? Was it just wishful thinking? Had too much wine and beer muddled my perceptions?

The two Georges rose from their chairs and quietly left. That was unusual for them. Like many of our friends, they liked to stay up drinking till the booze was gone. There was still a bottle of whiskey on the table. Rick helped Cathy up and led her to the spare bedroom. To me she looked as unaffected as one of the plump white dumplings on top of the stew I'd made for dinner. The aquarium she'd been blocking from view was suddenly visible and lit from within by its narrow band of lights along the lid. "Oh, no!" Patrick said. "The fish." En masse, they floated belly-up in the tank behind the woman I'd tried to destroy. The only things in the water that had survived were the snails. As before, they inched up the glass and down again, harvesting algae, unfazed, or so it seemed, by the dead bodies drifting around them.

An hour later, Rick woke up Patrick and said they had to drive Cathy to the hospital. She was having a nervous breakdown. Patrick left the house with them, and it was almost morning when he slipped into our bed beside me. Cathy had been booked into the psych ward, Patrick said. Rick was staying with her and on her insistence, he'd phoned her husband, who would be flying in late afternoon the following day to take her home. This was not the first of her nervous collapses. Their reading, scheduled for the evening, had to be cancelled.

I hadn't wanted to kill the fish. I felt bad about that, as I scooped them up with a small net—we'd have to replace them before our generous landlord found out—but I didn't feel guilty about Cathy. She was lucky to be alive.

In the four decades that have gone by since, I've tried to resurrect that paranormal power, I swear to use it for good not bad, but I've never been able to tap into it again. Just as well, perhaps. At literary festivals and at workshops over the years, would-be poets, fans, and students flirted outrageously with Patrick, and some of them made their availability obvious even when I was there. One crawled naked through his window at a workshop he was teaching outside of Sooke. Another dumped her husband and kids and showed up at our house in Saskatoon. She was going to live with Patrick as her guru and lover. It was okay, she said, if I stuck around. Who knows what I would have done had I been able? Now my short-lived telekinetic talent has become just another story. "Remember the time you killed the fish?" Patrick asks.

RECIPES

At the dinner party the woman
who intends to make love to my husband
tried to give me a recipe.
I have too many now, ones
I've saved for years from magazines
as if they're messages
of love or wisdom
that will teach me how to live.
They spill from drawers,
from the pockets of my bathrobe,
the pages of my books. Still
she persists, reciting
the ingredients: smoked salmon,
a cup of cream, lemon,
green onions, garlic and basil.
You'll love it, she says,
and don't hold back—
it's the spices
that make all the difference.
Later when we're home
exchanging stories about the party
before we go to bed,
he says her name out loud,
three times
in the course of conversation
as if he likes the sound of it,
as if he savours each
creamy vowel, each piquant
consonant on his tongue.

I am brushing my teeth.
I pretend I haven't noticed.
At least, I tell myself,
I'll know if he's been with her—
the smell of garlic
where her fingers swept across his belly
just below the navel
the oh so delicate taste of
basil on his skin.

Those years when Patrick and I entertained death at our table in a light-hearted way, thinking the shadowy figure would leave with the other guests long before dawn, one of our games was to collect epitaphs for each other. Our rules were that those worthy of consideration must be pithy one-liners, must bear the essence of the speaker's character, must feel natural and informal and be light enough to sound inconsequential, less weighty than what you'd expect for an *in memoriam*. They had to slip into a conversation that had nothing to do with last words, their context entirely different, yet they had to be able to survive an eternity in stone. Patrick has two in store for me. One is "Tomorrow I'm going to buy a ticket to somewhere."

The other comes from a night we spent on the farm of our friends Brian Brett and Sharon Doobenen on Salt Spring Island. In their flamboyant way, the two were hosting a huge party—there must have been sixty people milling around the acreage, drinks in hand. While dozens were bunked in their large log house, we'd been given the guests-of-honour sleeping quarters, a canvas teepee in the far corner of the yard. Earlier in the day, Patrick had helped Brian bury a butchered pig in burning coals deep in the ground.

That evening, after hours of feasting and several rounds of whiskey, Patrick had had enough. He crawled through the opening of the teepee and into the sleeping bags. Not long after, I wiggled in and snuggled beside him, the shouting and singing of serious revellers still going on outside. I asked, "Do you want to talk?" No. "Do you want to fuck?" No. "If you don't want to talk and you don't want to fuck, I'm going back to the party." This last sentence is what Patrick has threatened to hang over my grave. If he carries out his threat, I don't know what the grandkids will think.

The epitaph I've hung onto for him had its origins at a Lane family reunion in the Okanagan. It was going to be a complicated gathering. His ex-wife, who was pregnant at their grade-twelve graduation; the three kids from that marriage—all adults now, with their own children; his second ex-wife and their two teenage sons; Patrick's sister and two brothers with their spouses, and a swarm of nephews and nieces were all gathering to celebrate his mother's seventy-fifth birthday. Patrick called her "the Black Widow." Though he loved spiders, he didn't mean it as a compliment. She liked to sit at the centre of the Lane web and pluck the strings, making everyone jump, withdraw, or come near depending on her wishes. Sometimes, for your own good, it was best to balance on a thread as far out on the circumference as you could get. For me, that meant staying at our house in Saskatoon and sending him into the family fray by himself.

Only hours into the reunion on a hot, dry afternoon, crazy-drunk and stoned and dying to escape from his mother's machinations and the intimacies and guilt of two broken families, Patrick leapt off a twenty-five-foot cliff and dropped into the Shuswap River. This, at least, is the story he told me later. He'd seen a bunch of kids flying through the air and yelled at his four sons and his nephews to follow him in his running leap and plummet into the water below. He landed short, felt his ankle crunch and several of his vertebrae crack. He shouted to the rest of them, "Land farther out!" He was fifty years old. The muddy, soft shore and bottom of the river broke his fall somewhat but I don't know what, along with that, saved him from death or paralysis.

On his way to the operating room in Salmon Arm, where a surgeon would drill thirteen screws into his ankle, the orderly paused the gurney at the pay phone in the hall so he could speak to me in Saskatoon. He didn't say "I shouldn't have done it." Or, "I shouldn't have been drunk and stoned." Or even, "Boy was I lucky." Instead he said, "I should've jumped further, Babe." This is the man I love, I thought, when I heard those words. And they will be his epitaph.

From SOMEONE MUST BE DROWNING

It's easy to learn how to hold a funeral:
the bluebottle flies, the grieving wind, any number
of pines will tell you. But how to live one day!

## May, 2018

I'VE BEEN VISITING the isolation ward, masked, gloved, and gowned, for two three-hour periods daily; often I just sit by Patrick's bed and watch him sleep, my eyes shifting over the features I know so well. I trace an invisible line across his forehead, run it down one cheekbone and over the rise and underside of his chin, as if I need to imprint his face in the whorls of my fingertips. When he wakes up and sees me, we talk about small things: what the cats are doing, what's blooming in the garden, what I'll be having for supper, the kind of inconsequential details you can share only with someone you've been with a long time. Anyone else would be bored. One of the cats left a portly rat by the outdoor compost bin yesterday morning and perhaps the same one dropped a wounded mouse in the front hall. I didn't have the courage to stomp on it or stun it with whatever would do the job; instead I scooped it up in a dishcloth and tossed it outside in the laurel hedge. Something to atone for, I tell Patrick. If he'd been there, he'd have killed it cleanly and well. There'd have been no extended suffering. His no-nonsense, tender toughness is one of the things I fancy about him.

We say "I love you" at least five times a visit but after forty years, what else is there to say? The felicities of speech have vanished. Were they ever there? What did we talk about in the days before this distressing vigil began? In my memory, more powerful than our conversations were the silences, narrow grassy peninsulas that stretched between noisy waves of talking. We both found our feet there, we walked side by side, words taken away by the wind, and heard the deep quiet of each other. What a blessing is the absence of a need for utterance, what a comfort. Surely the quality of the silence, the knowing and the respect that it implies, is one of the things that makes people stay together. That and cats.

The first house we bought as a couple was an old two-storey on a small lot near the big Catholic cathedral in Regina. I'd been offered the writer-in-residence position at the library. I've never thought until now that in our first two cities, Winnipeg and Regina, we lived close to significant religious buildings that anchored the neighbourhoods. The one in Regina was in a part of town blighted with derelict older houses and slouched apartment buildings, some looking as if they'd been shelled in some long-ago, forgotten war. Our mortgage was $35,000 and we were terrified to take it on. This was 1981. We'd been together for three years. Though we didn't have steady jobs, the banker whom we had to see to get approval for the loan, a middle-aged, round-shouldered man in the requisite jacket and tie, took a chance on us when we told him what we did, because, he said, he'd always wanted to be a poet. He'd been praised in school for his poetry, but he'd never gone back to it. Instead he'd taken the safe route and studied accounting. He envied us, he said. This was the second financial beneficence poetry brought our way.

After we painted every room, tore up the worn orange carpets and sanded the floors with a big industrial machine that tried to tear itself out of Patrick's hands and roar up the walls and ceiling; after we bought a second-hand bed and a table and a couch and stacked the cupboards with pots and dishes from the Sally Ann; after we planted tomatoes, peas, and cucumbers in the narrow plot that was the garden, Patrick said, "I think you need a pet." I resisted. He'd never seen me with an animal, I warned him. I'd had three dogs. There was no separation between them and me. I was obsessed, neurotically so. "A cat, then," he said. "You can keep a distance with a cat."

"I don't want one."

"Let's just look," he said.

A sign hung above the door of the farthest room in the corridor at the Regina SPCA: "Last chance." It was four in the afternoon. We were told that by eight a.m. the next day, any cats that remained would be killed. My eyes swung past fifteen or so cages and stopped at a pair of yellow eyes in a wide tabby head. The card clipped on the wire mesh declared: Male, Stray, Two years to three years old. "What does it mean when an animal looks at you?" John Berger asked. I couldn't leave without this cat.

"You choose," Patrick said.

He was smaller than he first appeared, his head disproportionate to his body. Stretched out on my lap in the car, he fit with just his front paws hanging over. When we got him home, our first cat in our first mortgaged house, he leapt onto the kitchen counter and sniffed around the cap of the gin bottle. "We'll call him Nowlan," Patrick said. The New Brunswick poet, journalist, and short-story writer Alden Nowlan had died a year before. We loved his poetry and he'd loved gin. Patrick, who'd considered him his friend, had gotten drunk with him several times when he'd been on tour in the Maritimes. "Nowlan," we said, "welcome home."

## DOMESTIC SCENE

I mop the floors, admire again the grain,
the beautiful simplicity of wood.
The cat we named Nowlan after the poet
who just died, cries for his tin of fish.
You stuff our salmon with wild rice
and watercress, its flesh pink
as Nowlan's mouth, his perfect tongue.
How lucky we are to have found each other,
our fine grey cat, a fresh Atlantic salmon.
Tomorrow we may get drunk and fight
or buy two tickets to Madrid.
But tonight the light in our kitchen
is as good as any you'll find anywhere.
The plates glow with possibilities
and the cat licks himself completely clean.

Nowlan's small size was no indication of his daring. He'd strut along the tall wooden fence that separated our back yard from the neighbour's and drive the nasty Rottweiler berserk, slicing the air with his front claws just above the reach of the leaping dog's blunt head. Though mostly affectionate and calm with us, sometimes Nowlan would give us a look that meant he was about, for no reason we could understand, to spring and attack, sinking his teeth into an elbow or a knee. "Uh-oh, that look again," one of us would say, and Patrick or I would drop our gaze and walk away.

Nowlan lived with us for fourteen years, uneasily adjusting to five different houses. He was most unhappy and out of place when he came with us to Montreal, where Patrick took on a residency at

Concordia. We joked that he couldn't speak *joual* to the alley cats and they picked on him. Or that, in trying this new dialect of meows, he made mistakes that came out sounding like insults from this feline westerner who had no élan. Night after night he jumped through the window into our bedroom from the fire escape, beat-up and sullen; but he wouldn't be kept inside. He'd streak past our legs whenever the door opened. There was business to be taken care of in the alleys.

Shortly after our time in Montreal, we moved from Regina to Saskatoon, to share a position teaching every second fall at the university. In one of our years off, we were offered a residency at the University of Toronto, Patrick taking one semester and me the next. Nowlan's bad Montreal experience made us decide to leave him at the house in Saskatoon, an old three-storey Victorian within walking distance of the campus. For some reason we were compelled, wherever we lived, to buy a house. Lucky for us this compulsion to take on a mortgage was limited, so far, to Saskatchewan, where prices were some of the lowest in the country. Who knew either of us, unconventional in other ways, were such nesters? Having to rent out our place when we were in Toronto, we wanted a tenant who'd take care of our home but, more importantly, take good care of Nowlan.

I posted a notice on the bulletin board in the halls of the English Department, hoping for a doctoral student or a sessional lecturer needing digs for the academic year. Instead a young man from the vet college phoned and tried to set up an interview. "Not interested in male students," I said. I told him about the house my ex-husband had shared with two buddies, one in law school and one in medicine, when we were in university. Within the first week of classes, it had become party central. You'd have sworn it had been decorated by Bob and Doug McKenzie. You couldn't get near the sink for all the beer bottles and greasy pizza boxes and piles of unidentified garbage, not even bagged. No one did the dishes or bothered to make the short trip to the trash bin. You didn't want to consider the mattresses, the toilets, the stiff towels in the bathroom, the smell.

The vet student and his friend showed up at our door anyway. Dressed in white shirts and skinny ties, they shook my hand and passed on reference letters from three professors. Both looked so fresh and sincere. The shorter of the two said, "This is our last year. Our courses are harder than med school's—we don't have time for parties." The other one said, "Besides, who would take better care of your cat?" Nowlan brushed against his leg and looked on with what seemed to be amusement and approval. I've always read too much in the expressions of cats.

The two vets-to-be put down a huge deposit, paid the first and last months' rent, and signed a contract that ensured they'd pay for damages. It wouldn't have held up in a court of law, but once we'd made the decision, it made us feel better. We packed the car and headed off for Toronto, Patrick in a cast from ankle to hip because of his leap off the cliff into the Shuswap River. Our car was a stick shift. I did the driving until we hit Manitoba and my back gave out, spasms shooting from my sacrum and down my left leg. Long drives had always been bad for me, but I'd never felt these tasers of pain before. Patrick had to take over as I hunched like a crab in the passenger's seat, him stopping every hour so I could lie on the shoulder of the highway and pull my right knee, then the left, to my chest, the way the chiropractor had shown me. We both prayed he wouldn't have to move his heavy, plaster-encased ankle and leg to slam on the brake. The traffic on the 401 was harrowing; I don't know how we made it.

From IF I CALL STONES BLUE

Today a letter
arrived from the cat. I'm okay
in Saskatoon without you though
I prefer your lap. He always says
the right thing, that cat.

On our return eight months later, the house was immaculate, the only thing broken an antique ceiling light fixture at the bottom of the stairs. Had someone leapt right into it from the landing and shattered it to pieces? It was obvious our tenants had hired a maid service to scrub from top to bottom. Scattered on the floor were wool mice filled with catnip, probably knit and stuffed by one of their mothers. Nowlan looked somewhat bored to see us but he deigned to let me pick him up and bury my nose in his soft belly the colour of a ripe peach. There was a note thanking us for our trust and hoping we found everything to our liking. Nowlan was okay, we had no complaints; we mailed them their damage deposit.

Our next move with Nowlan, a year later, was to Saanichton, a bedroom community outside of Victoria where I took up a tenure-track position teaching in the writing department at the university. We had decided that fifteen years of living off our writing wits was enough—they were wearing thin. One of us needed a steady job, and I was the one with a master's degree. Besides, the department had made it known that they had to hire a woman. I would be the first.

A few blocks away from our new house was a big animal clinic that saved money on staff salaries by hiring recent graduates willing to work for starting wages. The closest vet college was in

Saskatoon. The first time we took Nowlan in for his shots, a white-jacketed young woman just out of school, someone we'd never seen before, walked into the examining room, saw him and did a double take. "Nowlan, sweetheart, what are you doing here?"

"You know Nowlan?" I asked.

"Oh, yeah, Nowlan's a great cat. We used to party at his house all the time."

This scene replayed two more times when we took him to that clinic. "Nowlan, old buddy, where'd you come from?" a young man asked.

"Nowlan, is that you? Give me five!" another said, happy for his reunion with the party cat.

When I visit the hospital, I don't bring diversions—unlike the woman in Patrick's first room, who sat beside her husband and worked on puzzles in a crossword book, the kind you find near the cash register in grocery stores. Although we've played crib in the past, for some reason I've resisted arriving with a crib board and a deck of cards. It would seem a fake solace, and more than that, a surrendering, an acceptance that he's going to be here a long time, trapped in the prison of his body, bored, querulous; a life sentence, a death sentence hanging over his head.

A couple of friends have dropped off books, ones I wouldn't mind taking home and dipping into. Patrick hasn't opened them. He is too confused and ill to follow another writer's characters or plot, so I've decided to read out loud from his new novel, *Deep River Night*. In what now seems like a miracle, at least a miracle of dedication and belief in one's vocation, Patrick, wired on a steroid to treat his mysterious disease, worked on his next-to-last draft after his bout in the hospital last February. Though he's suffered from cognitive confusion and his brain, in his words, has "felt like a heavy, wet towel," he needed to do a final editing that included creating a new opening chapter. Confronted by this advice from his editor, he said, "I'm going to send back the advance and tell them I can't do it."

"You can delay this," I said. "You're the boss, not the publisher. Just leave it for a few weeks and see how you feel." His editor pushed him by making him feel guilty for even considering giving up and by believing in the beauty of the writing on the pages she'd received. "I've already spent a hundred hours on this," she said. "It's too brilliant to stop now." I felt so grateful she was able to convince him to finish the book when I couldn't. I watched him, released from the hospital but not his illness, day after day go into his office and hunch over his computer. I never asked how it was going. I never asked to read a word. My interest, my interference, could have shattered everything.

Now the book is in my hands. The writing so gorgeous, the diction so rich, as I read to him out loud, I have to force myself to keep moving from sentence to sentence rather than stopping and exclaiming in wonder and praise. God, this man can craft a word, a phrase, a paragraph, a chapter, a book! And the pages shine with the kind of hard-won wisdom that can come only from a writer with over seven decades behind him. How does this person I live with, who appears so ordinary in our daily lives as he shops for groceries, does the laundry, cleans the litter box, clips the perennials in the garden, tames the cat—how does he see so clearly, how does he know so much?

It seems to relax him, my reading of his words, and I peer over the cover of the novel and watch his face, so dear to me, on the standard, faded-blue hospital pillow. His eyes flutter under his closed eyelids as if he were re-envisioning image after image on the page, the things he saw in his inner mind and jigged into language. "The dark cup of the cat's ear moved, the long guard hairs at the tip shivering toward the crack in the window beside her. Art finished his drink, put his glass down by the whiskey bottle, and waited to see if the cat's ear would come back to rest, but it didn't." His words curl off my tongue with exquisite, demanding exactitude, each a tribute to the courtesy and attention he affords to the things around him, the working men and women he grew up with, the hardness of the life, and the various creatures that populate his rich and teeming imagination; in this case, a cat.

The only thing that brings me as much pleasure is curling up beside him on top of the thin bedspread, my head resting on his shoulder, my top leg swung over his. I've taken off the gloves and mask, hoping I won't get caught by the staff and upbraided. "This is the best part," he says. I close my eyes until the nurse comes into the room with his medication for the night. She seems bemused to see two old people snuggled together among the tubes and monitors that register his blood pressure, heart rate, oxygen level. There is nothing amorous about this room. It is the epitome of anti-romance. But the bed is the same size as the one where we spent our first nights together when Patrick moved into my room at the Summer School of the Arts in the old TB sanitarium in Fort Qu'Appelle.

For a moment, I wonder if the tuberculosis virus that attacked so many had lurked in the corners of those old corridors of patients' rooms and crawled into his nose or mouth. Did it lie in wait in his bloodstream and, decades later, overrun the country of his body? It can't be. It's just coincidence that the bed feels the same, so different from the queen-sized we sleep in at home. I am amazed the narrow hospital cot feels just the right width as I nestle next to him as if, in his sickness, we've both become smaller.

When everything else is gone, will this diminished, worn-out thing we are together be all that will remain? There's a sweetness in this and a sadness and something I can't put my finger on. *Where do I go from here? Am I supposed to help you? The windows are wrong.*

Everything between us is stretched thin and fragile as an old person's skin. Everything bruises. We've both pondered which one of us will have to help the other out of this life, which one will be left alone. I don't want to be the one abandoned. And I know he doesn't want to be, too. The nine years' difference in our ages didn't mean anything when we met; it means something now. I'm more than likely to be the caregiver, the one left behind, the one who has to walk miles and miles through staggering grief, carrying an unbearable emptiness on my back.

### FINALLY

The word *love* means someone takes you
in your old clothes, your face too bare, too open,
when someone fastens the buttons on your coat
as if you've fallen back through sixty years to be
a child again, when someone takes you onto the path,
holding you by the arm, your feet not knowing what
they used to know, your feet in rubber boots stumbling,
blind to roots and stones, when someone takes you
to the ocean, the water also raining down
its saltless weeping. The word *love* means someone
takes you to the rocks, rain too heavy for the gulls
to lift, three bobbing like windless boats, all sails
and heartbeat, love leaves you there, no words
for it now, you and the gulls and the ocean
that moves as far away from you as it can go.

When we were both well, we talked about what we'd like done with us after death. My mother was the model for that: in the never-used teapot in the china cabinet she left a list of things for my brother and me, including the number to call to apply for a modest benefit from the credit union where she'd banked all her adult life, directions for the scattering of her ashes, and her instructions for a funeral: "I don't want one!" She also insisted on the shortest of obituaries to ever be published in the local paper: "Peggy Crozier is gone."

My mother was the most practical, non-sentimental woman I've ever met. That had its drawbacks. I vividly remember the night she decided to settle with my father what he wanted done with his body after he died. "Tell Lorna while she's here," she said, "and while you still have your druthers." Dad looked as taken aback as I felt. I was visiting for a few days, and we were sitting in their living room, watching *Hockey Night in Canada*. Dad had been about to leave for the bar in one of the downtown hotels. He wasn't a hockey fan; that was Mom's game. He liked to watch wrestling.

"I don't know," he finally said, for once not impatient to be gone.

She told him she was going to be cremated and did he want that too? "There's no sense in buying real estate in graveyards," she continued. "That's just a waste of money we don't have, and besides, with the kids so far away there'll be no one to take care of the plots and they'll just go all weedy. Or a gopher will dig us up." Dad agreed—how could he not?—cremation would be the best thing. "Then what should we do with your ashes?" she asked.

"You could hire a plane," Dad said, "and drop them over the roof of the house."

"That's just like you," Mom said, "to think of something so expensive. I'm not paying for a plane. And besides, I don't want you hanging over my head on the roof the rest of my life." She shot down his next idea too—to be planted in the garden. "No way. I'd be tasting you every time I ate a carrot." He finally agreed to go where she was going: to the spring that fed into the big alkali lake on the farm where she'd grown up, the drought-prone land just across the road from the Crozier property.

For Patrick and me, as for my parents, cremation seems the best option since we're not connected to a church or feel we'd be at home in any nearby graveyard. If I were on my own, I might choose to return to the maternal farm in Saskatchewan, where my parents' fire-eaten remains have sunk into the salt-encrusted water or been tongued and eaten by the wind. Patrick might choose Okanagan Lake, where he swam as a child, or the Vernon cemetery, where his mother, father, niece, and older brother are buried. But we've both said we want our bones—at least what's left of them—to lie together, to intermingle and become one nameless, fleshless nothingness in the earth.

We've talked about scattering our charred morsels into the ocean—after all, we live across from a bay that belongs to the Pacific—but the idea makes me shiver. As much as I love it, I'm not an ocean person; I find it cold and forbidding. A compromise is the grove of trees we painstakingly cleared of ivy, though with Patrick too ill to attack the vines with his saw and secateurs and me worn out from running the house on my own, the ivy's crept back. We knew it would be a never-ending task, but we didn't know the day so soon would come when we wouldn't be up for it. On most of the trees we freed from infestation, ivy snakes up the trunks. On several, it's already four feet high. It hurts to see it.

To the south of one of the two walkways leading to the bay lies a shallow concavity at the base of an old mother fir. Nearby a bridge crosses a narrow stream you can hear running over stones in the rainy season when you sit under the tree, and in front, there's a path the deer have stamped through the greenery. I'm sure it's been a deer trail longer than we've been alive. Here, we've decided, what's left of us will mingle, we'll find each other ash by ash, bone shard by bone shard, memory by memory, even if we die years apart. What will grow from the two of us in the uncaring rain will be different from what would grow from one of us alone. If we're lucky it will be an offspring of the tree that's lasted more than a hundred years and that towers a hundred feet into the sky. Maybe, considering the jests of the gods, what will thrive will be ivy.

A GOOD PLACE

A forest draped
        with moss and mist—
a softness,
        a quietude—
a good place to send the soul.

When Patrick and I collided—our meeting was akin to nuclear fusion, one friend wrote—I was passion's ad agent. I'd say to anyone who'd listen that you shouldn't settle for a life without it, that nothing else can take its place: not friendship, security, not mutual respect. You need those as well, I guess, but I'd insist that love without passion is tepid, and surely you want to burn. "Hot blood, hot thoughts, hot deeds": we could have used these words from Shakespeare's *Troilus and Cressida* as a litany—they matched what we felt when we met.

We found a resonance, too, in the advice of one of the desert fathers whose teachings and sayings Thomas Merton translated and published in 1960. The book came with Patrick when we met, included in the bundle of the few possessions he couldn't bear to leave behind. The story goes like this: A monk makes the long trek to seek help from an old master, who lives as a hermit in the desiccated wasteland. The younger monk says he's done all the right things: he's sacrificed, he's changed his life, he's been a good man, why hasn't he reached enlightenment? The wise one shrugs and says, "Why not be changed to fire?" The master surely meant the pure fire of spiritual illumination, but could he also have been alluding to the fire of passion? Years into our lives together, when we were feeling dull, out of sorts, caught in a tedium of our own making, one of us might ask, "Why not be changed to fire?" The embers could still flare with a challenge, a glance, a touch.

About twelve years ago, when I was in my late fifties, I was compelled to look at the physical side of our relationship through different eyes. After being asked to write a poem for a Sidney fundraiser that billed itself as a night of erotica, I ran into a kind of writer's block I hadn't encountered before. It was tall and wide and constructed of glass bricks that reflected my aging body back to me. In the past, I'd had no trouble generating so-called erotic poems, most of them humorous, for such events. Suddenly I couldn't do it. Although I could have parroted Shirley Hazzard's observation in her novel *The Great Fire*, "I realise, too, that I now have a substantial past—which means that I am no longer young but have become more interesting to myself," my more interesting self shied away from exposing on the page all this sun-damage and slippage. Finding words was hard enough but my cheeks burned when I thought of presenting such a thing on stage in this reconstituted grandmotherly form that had suddenly become me.

When I could see the amusing side of this new stage of my physical mutation, my self-consciousness and fear of ridicule became, in the end, the inspiration for what I called "My Last Erotic Poem." I'd hoped the title was tongue-in-cheek.

## EROTIC POEM

s to hear about
two old farts getting it on
in the back seat of a Buick,
in the garden shed among vermiculite,
in the kitchen where we should be drinking
ovaltine and saying no? Who wants to hear
about 26 years of screwing,
our once-not-unattractive flesh
now loose as unbaked pizza dough
hanging between two hands before it's tossed?

Who wants to hear about two old lovers
slapping together like water hitting mud,
hair where there shouldn't be
and little where there should,
my bunioned foot sliding
up your bony calf, your calloused hands
sinking in the quickslide of my belly,
our faithless bums crepitous, collapsed?

We have to wear our glasses to see down there!

When you whisper what you want I can't hear,
but do it anyway, and somehow get it right. Face it,
some nights we'd rather eat a Häagen-Dazs ice cream bar
or watch a movie starring Nick Nolte who looks worse than us.
Some nights we'd rather stroke the cats.

Who wants to know when we get it going
we're revved up, like the first time—honest—
like the first time, if only we could remember it,
our old bodies doing what you know
bodies do, worn and beautiful and shameless.

I presented the poem as part of my new work at various events and literary festivals, but not when Patrick was in the room. He'd asked me not to. It made him squirm with embarrassment, he said. He, more than anyone else, should have seen the hyperbole in the images—we weren't as decrepit as I made us out to be—but he didn't budge until I launched the book that included that poem at Harbourfront's International Festival of Authors in Toronto. By then, we were almost a decade older—even more worn and shameless than the characters I'd described.

We were on the same bill at Harbourfront. He was presenting his novel *Red Dog, Red Dog* in a lineup with three other novelists, and I, as the only poet, had been asked to give a ten-minute warm-up. With his permission I read the poem, saving it till the end and having to pause several times because of the audience's laughter in the darkened, sold-out room. Patrick went to the mic right after me, but before he opened his novel, he said, "You know I'm on the road a lot this fall, promoting this book, and before tonight, I used to worry about Lorna, me leaving her by herself so much, I thought she'd be lonely. Now I realize I shouldn't have been worried—she's been having an affair with some old guy." The crowd broke up, not settling down to listen for about five minutes. Touché, my darling, I thought.

———

He was wearing a short-sleeved black t-shirt and jeans hitched to his waist with a worn brown belt. I hooked my fingers around its leather, burrowed my nose in that spot where the neck meets the collarbone and breathed him in—the smell of summer sunshine and cigarettes and that particular odour that I've come to recognize as him—my new lover, my man. Having read Lord Byron at university, did I recall his line, "I knew it was love, and I felt it was glory"? I like to think so.

Patrick arrived at the Fort San summer school to sweep me away. It was 1978. After four years of being a student there, I'd been asked to teach. Patrick drove hundreds of miles from the Sunshine Coast through the B.C. and Alberta mountains and across the prairies to drop into this small valley he'd never heard of before. He had to find it, with difficulty, on a map and stop at a gas station east of Regina to ask for help. He parked his car in the gravel lot, asked a kid carrying a trumpet where the writers were housed, found the building, demanded of a stranger inside, "Where's Lorna?" and strode to the room where I was sitting on the edge of a student's cot going over her poem. He said, "Come with me." Without speaking, I followed him to his car. He leaned against the door and, in the parlance of a romance novel, I fell into his arms.

He told the woman who ran the school that he was just passing through. She was thrilled that Patrick Lane had dropped in. "Will you give a reading before you go?" she asked and showed him to a vacant room on the ground floor in the writers' dorm. At first no one knew why he'd stopped in this out-of-the-way place on the way to somewhere else, but it didn't take them long to figure it out. He boldly dropped his bag by my bed on the second floor, not bothering to pretend to occupy the space he'd been given. Well into the week, when I arrived in the downstairs lounge to start my morning workshop, one of the younger students complained that the person staying above her kept jumping up and down on the bed and woke her up every night and early morning. A red flush rose up my neck and blazed my cheeks. She didn't know it was my room she was talking about, and she was too naïve to realize it was the bed that was jumping because of the couple in it, not another student reverting to a rambunctious childhood stunt.

Fort San was the perfect setting for the start of what we both admitted later might have been just a summer fling. There was a magic to the place, the kind that creativity casts on otherwise conventional people. Like me they'd all left something behind— jobs, duties, spouses, children. The green valley that suddenly appeared as if a giant cleaver had swung from the sky and sliced into the flatness separated them from what was going on above, from where they worked and worshipped and raised their families. When they left the highway and dropped to the bottom of the coulees, they were falling into a different element, a strange and foreign land.

For three blissful summer weeks at the school of the arts, orthodoxies were abandoned. Even your skin tingled with inspiration as thirty or so writers scribbled away in their small, cell-like rooms, and a primal, sexual energy danced in the air like dust motes in the beams of sunshine that poured in the windows and buffed Echo Lake into a blue satin sheen. On summer nights, a gang of poets roared down the road the five miles to the Squire Hotel in Fort Qu'Appelle in the back of a half-ton truck like the small-town high school kids we used to be, singing "Cigarettes and whisky and wild, wild women" under the brightest stars in the world. In a circle we danced until the band left the stage and the barkeep yelled

"Last call." In the early years, Rudy Wiebe was with us, equally as boisterous, though he drank Tang, the only non-alcoholic fruit drink the bar served, and he didn't dance.

The setting, the vibrancy of artists crammed together—writers, musicians, dancers, painters—fireworked through that verdant valley and lit up the mind and flesh. Stripped of custom, of normal daily tasks, we all became a little wilder. That wildness showed up in poems and stories, in the dancing at the pubs, the songs around the campfires, and sometimes in affairs. When others carried on at the school, at least in my experience, the liaisons were clandestine. People slipped furtively at night into another's bed and pretended almost convincingly during the day that they weren't involved. Looking back at it now, I can't believe that Patrick and I were so daring and indiscreet. Everyone knew we were married to other people, yet Patrick simply showed up, out of the blue you could say, and occupied my room.

Part of the brazenness came from his character—his candour, his confidence. This was a man who knew what he wanted and who refused to be ashamed or diverted by the possible outrage of others. If something felt right to him, he did it without looking over his shoulder or glancing back. In his book *The Marriage of Cadmus and Harmony*, the Italian novelist Roberto Calasso distinguishes between Dionysus and weavers. He explains that the former "is not a useful god who helps weave or knot things together, but a god who loosens and unties. The weavers are his enemies. Yet there comes a moment when the weavers will abandon their looms to dash off after him into the mountains. Dionysus is the river we hear flowing by in the distance, an incessant booming from far away." When Patrick arrived at the school the river's booming came closer. The waters rose and flooded my room, carrying me away.

From GOLDEN AND THE RIVER

At daybreak he left Golden and the river
dipping into the canyon. A mountain range
to cross and then the foothills,
the long, unrolling plains before the valley
and linked lakes of Qu'Appelle.

That morning I didn't know
where he'd started from or when
but I felt something different on my skin
as I walked the shore of Echo Lake—
the wake of his car in the wind 800 miles away
stirred the air around me.

That summer "It's a Heartache" blared
from every radio, Bonnie Tyler's throat
full of coke and come. I could see him in the car
caught inside the song, the greedy gut of heat,
fingers drumming the wheel, black T-shirt
wet with sweat, pulled tight across his chest.
The button on his jeans could burn a finger.


On top of the mysterious attack of his body on his body, the doctors finally diagnosed the source of the infection that made Patrick
crash and brought him so close to death—pneumonia. I can't help
but think of its sobriquet: "an old man's blessing," called that
because it ends the suffering of the elderly and ill quickly, mercifully, I guess. The other day, his two sons who live in Victoria walked

through the door of his room, gowned and masked. I could tell from the look on Patrick's face that he didn't recognize them. They could have been doctors. "Hi, Michael. Hi, Richard," I said loudly so Patrick could hear. "We didn't know you were coming."

"Why don't you go home?" Michael said. "We'll watch him now."

"He doesn't need to be watched, but I'll go home and you can visit." I bent over the bed and kissed Patrick on the lips. "Your germs are my germs," I told him. And my heart, your heart, I didn't say out loud. Your body, my body, though we are two people, not one.

While Patrick's been away, the garden is, indeed, going on without him. I feel quite helpless in the face of its demands. We've had a division of labour in our lives, something which I now regret. Advice to a daughter I never had: we should have split the same task, not delegated one thing to me and another to him. I don't know how to set the timer for the irrigation system, scatter the exact amount of fertilizer on the Scottish moss that carpets the area around the pond (too much will burn it), clean the filter in the pump, prune the roses so the bushes keep their elegant shapes. I can't find the phone number of the guy who services the lawn tractor, or the name of the electrician who's supposed to fix the lighting system in the front yard; I don't know where Patrick filed our house insurance or our wills. I don't know which bills are paid automatically and which I have to take care of with a cheque. Though I can reach the pot light in the kitchen ceiling with the stepladder, my fingers aren't strong enough to turn the burned-out bulb and pull it out. If I twist too hard will I break it and cut my hands? I can't even change a fucking lightbulb.

And then there's Basho. I'm the one who holds him, Patrick the one who inserts the needle for his twice-a-week injections of intravenous water. I can't make myself do it. I'm afraid I'll puncture a muscle or hit a bone and really hurt him. Po Chu's a problem for a different reason. She needs to be taken to the vet for her yearly shots but, unlike Patrick, I can't pick her up without fear of getting slashed. I thought I was an independent woman but really I'm a wimp, a bumbling idiot who needs a strong man to keep the household going. I'm so frustrated with my helplessness that I feel like kicking a hole in the wall. But then who would fix it?

Yesterday the locum filling in for our regular doctor, who'd given up her hospital rounds because her ninety-year-old mother was dying, popped into Patrick's room and asked, "Have you two discussed do-not-resuscitate?" We were both stunned, partly because she asked so casually, as if she was querying whether Patrick wanted to accept or refuse the fake whipped-cream topping on the cubes of Jell-O that gleamed and wiggled like Martian victuals on his supper tray. "We'll do everything we can to make him live," she said, "but does he want to be on a ventilator for instance or get his heart shocked with paddles?"

"No," he replied in a weak voice. "I don't want that." And I told her we'd had the pull-the-plug conversation many times in the past and neither of us wanted extraordinary rescue measures, but the day after this too-brief exchange, I start to fret. He'd just been rescued from our home, he was unconscious, he couldn't talk or think or breathe with ease. If he fell into that state again, did it mean no one would help him? Would they let him die? I could see a big *DNR* clipped to his chart and a nurse simply walking away if he was in distress. I prayed Patrick wouldn't relapse over the weekend. I'd have to track the doctor down and get her to expunge those initials from the page. *Resuscitate*, I wanted to yell, *at any cost*.

On the wall board in his room, on his chart, on a tag hung around his neck I wanted to write in big red letters, *Save this man!*

Most people who meet Basho claim he's the most gorgeous cat they've ever seen. He went from a blue-eyed puff of cumulus you could hold in one hand to a long lean snow leopard who slipped with the sideways grace of that ephemeral creature out of sight through ropes of winter rain. His eyes were not the blue of an ordinary sky but the clearer, colder blue of heaven. Some days they took on the hue of a never-seen-before lake lost in the high mountains hooded with snow. You could not look into them without wondering what he was thinking, and you knew his thoughts were fierce and deep.

The colour of his coat too seemed to shift. It was mocha, then a breath of greyish smoke rising from a low valley, then a quickened silver mist when the morning sun caught its sheen. If for a moment you thought you were the superior species, you only had to glance at Basho winding his sleek beauty behind the fragile clay vase on a narrow shelf in our living room or leaping without wings or a trampoline six feet into the air and down to earth again. What he was leaping for, we were never sure, some falling slip of spirit we couldn't see.

We had named him well. The human Basho, born five centuries before his namesake, could have spent a lifetime trying to capture those graceful feline lines in the strokes of his calligraphy brushes. The human Basho, too, might have paused in his journey to his eternal far north to hang around with our cat and us for a day or two. He who coined such names as "Unreal Hut" and "Villa of Fallen Persimmons" could have helped us name our new gate. A life-sized ceramic crow perches on top of a pole beside it. We've thought of "Crow-Hesitating-to-Go-Through Gate." There's a circular frame, empty inside, made up of two halves, the bottom curve cut into the low swinging door. To make it more dramatic, the builder traced its rounded shape with a thin swipe of red paint. We've thought of "Full-Moon-But-the-Moon-Has-Gone Gate." Basho, I would ask, which one do you prefer?

Basho the poet might have helped us strip ivy in the forest across the road—after all, he had an affinity for trees, choosing his pen name from a banana sapling a student planted outside his hut. He loved the banana tree for its modesty—though it sometimes flowered, the blossoms were small—for the ephemerality of its leaves both green and brown at the same time, and for its lack of a practical use. Unlike pines or bamboo, it didn't know an axe, it wasn't cut for lumber or stakes. After planting shoots from the original to a new spot in his garden, he wrote, "Like the famous ancient tree of the mountains, the basho's useless nature is itself the reason to admire it. A monk caressed that mountain tree with his brush to learn its ways; a scholar watched its leaves unfold to inspire his studies. But I'm not like either of them. I just rest in the shade of the leaves I love because they are so easily torn."

Far from his hut, also named Basho, under the great limbs of cedar and fir, he would labour alongside us, tearing at the ivy, he in his monk's robes and an old straw hat. He'd haloed his head with poetry, writing around the sweat-stained rim: "Under this world's long rains, / here passes / poetry's makeshift shelter." Just a few days ago at a market for gardeners, I bought a pair of secateurs modelled after an ancient Japanese model. They fit my hand better than the common Swiss-made Felcos, but if you don't hold them correctly they pinch the web between your finger and thumb. I'd have shown Basho how to use them if he didn't already know.

After hours in the forest, before he went on his way—for he was always an intrepid traveller, walking twenty to thirty miles a day—we'd have served him tea in our gazebo. A small brown bat, as it had the summer before, might have dunked into the pond, then, hanging from the roof beam, stretched its wings to dry. The miniature shower it created would have dripped onto my elbow and Patrick's knee. Dripped, perhaps, onto Basho's hat. Four hundred years after his death, we'd sit quietly with him, taking in his silence and his heart-inspired gaze, his communion with the natural world. His namesake, too long to fit in the pilgrim poet's lap, stretched at his sandalled feet. The Master would have liked him there, the long cat hair warm and soft on his toes. Centuries ago the poet Basho told one of his students, trying to teach the younger acolyte respect for all worldly creatures, "Not: dragonfly; remove its wings—pepper tree. But: pepper tree; add wings to it—dragonfly." No one has said it better.

## Late May, 2018

PATRICK'S HOME FROM the hospital after a two-week stay that felt like a year—so much has shifted. They let him go not because he's well but because they don't know what else to do. He says he's just waiting for the next catastrophe. Pneumonia still whispering in his lungs, his blood counts low, he moves around the house only with the help of a walker that we borrowed from the place that makes those things available, who knew? It rattles and clanks as he pushes it and his weariness down the hall from room to room, a ghost, a ghost in chains.

He has the legs of a ten-year-old boy, his arms are smaller than mine. I once wrote a poem about the way he walked—"Even the dead reach for you / as you walk, so beautiful across the earth." It was a sexy, blue-jeaned, slim-hipped swagger, the assured gait of a man at home in his body and the world. Now it's a clank, slide, clank, slide, his legs capable of an uneasy balance, not power or confidence. The walker sits by our bed at night so he can make it the short distance from our bed to the bathroom. He uses it to navigate the paths of the garden, and often I see him motionless behind it as if it's a stubborn aluminum gate he can't figure out how to push through. I remind myself he'll get to the other side of it, but it will take time, it will take time. I ache for him.

If we'd had children, would our feelings about each other have been less intense? Do children temper the enchantment, water it down so that the paint runs thinner across the canvas of a long infatuation? I can't answer because we didn't have them, but I wonder now. When we got together, he had fathered five. I understood he didn't want any more. I felt bereft only briefly, around my mid-thirties when my body demanded a fragment of me to continue into the future, but right from the start I was aware that hooking up with Patrick gave me permission to do one of the most transgressive things for a woman in my society—not have children. Even in this century, it's radical to choose that option. Most men and women I know don't see it as an option at all. Falling for Patrick meant I'd be childless and that I'd pour everything I was and would be into something else.

I see him in the two sons I am close to, but I don't see me. Because we lived far away from them and moved so often, when they were little they visited rarely; their mother understandably held them close. We were allowed to be selfish, to put everything into our art and into each other. He is my world and I am his, and oh, that feels impossibly wrenching right now. If we'd had children . . .

As white blossoms flare on the rhododendron branches in our front yard, Patrick tells me he's ready to build the fence he started just before he collapsed and was rushed to the hospital while I was in Edmonton. In the past, I've admired his adeptness with a hammer and nails; his hands possess the elegance and sureness of a conductor's, a professional cellist's, a lover's who knows the hollows and rises of his woman's body. When he builds and repairs, there's no wasted movement, no misjudging of distance or timing. After he was admitted to the hospital (for his third time, his fourth?) I'd moved his power-saw, nails, and hammer—anything that could rust—into the carport out of the rain, but I left the sawhorses and lumber at the site, somehow thinking if I'd put everything away, it meant he wouldn't return to the task. He'd sunk the posts on the side of the front garden where the fence had collapsed and nailed in the top and bottom horizontals. Now the vertical palings, about twenty of them, need to be cut and hammered in place.

"You're not capable," I tell him. "You can't saw and pound nails, bend, get up, or even stand for any length of time."

"One board at a time," he says. "I'll build the fence one board at a time."

And that's what he does over the next few days. Goes outside, lines up a grey cedar board he salvaged from the old fence, measures it, draws a pencil mark, and saws off the rotten end. Rests against the sawhorses, moves with his walker, board in hand to the posts and beams, squats, pounds nails, and uses the skeleton of the fence to pull himself to his feet. I pretend I'm not watching. Sometimes he stays on his knees for what seems like a long time, then tries to push himself upright again. He falters, sways on his feet, but he makes it, just.

I know the courage it takes to do this simple task, the determination. The shell of his illness is thick and heavy on his back, a weight that looks insurmountable as he bends to hammer then struggles to stand upright. His left leg has no power at all. The muscles turned to mush. Rest. One board. Rest. The next day another board. And then it's too much. Three in place and the morning after, he can't heave himself out of bed. Still, I don't move the sawhorses or the salvaged palings waiting to be measured and cut. The gap-toothed fence waits for him to fill it in. This is my new image of a tormented and frail hope.

BEAUTY

It's not the antelope's
                golden leaps across the grasslands
but how she stops
drops to her knees at the barbed-wire fence
                                and crawls under
    then springs when she's on her feet again
So too with you. The beauty's in
        your fall, your startled
                    grace—
    everything
            turning on
the hinges of your neck, waist, and knees
                how you bend—


The diminutives he calls me: Little Bones, Little Bear, Pepper, My Moon Wolf, My Howler Monkey, Crow. The last because of my surname. He means it fondly, but when he loudly calls *Crow*, looking for me in the aisles of the hardware store or among the crowd at the farmers' market, we get odd looks. Is this how he sees her? strangers must think. Black-coated, raggedy old woman, hopping on stiff knees from spot to spot, hawking out croaks and caws—what an insult! My brother, in elementary school, used to beat kids up if they called him that. They'd stopped before I'd reached grade one, seven years later. Now, though, I find the name in my loved one's mouth endearing, the hard "C" and the long, drawn-out vowel—he's looking for me!—and don't mind being paired with the bird. In the mid-1800s the Reverend Henry Ward Beecher wrote, "If men had wings and bore black feathers, few of them would be clever enough to be crows." Patrick has faith in the potential corvid cleverness of me.

In the Royal Jubilee Hospital in central Victoria last fall, his fourth admittance in sixteen months, Patrick was assigned a room on the top floor. Every day around noon, a flotilla of crows flew past the big windows; so many it looked as if scraps of charred paper had exploded from the chimney of a beehive burner and blackened the sky. Hundreds and hundreds, I couldn't keep count. Around five o'clock they'd cross again, going the opposite direction. Their numbers and their remarkable determination to reach wherever it was they were going attested to the world and its creatures doggedly continuing outside of that room, outside of our worries and concerns. It made us think of W.H. Auden's ship which "sailed calmly on" while the boy Icarus fell into the sea.

The crows' mid-day destination might have been the ocean. It was close by, its shore a rich feeding ground. Countless times we'd watched them pick up clams from the beach and, hovering in the sky, drop them on rocks or pavement to crack open the shells. Maybe their starting point and the place they returned to late afternoon was a park with wide fir trees where they roosted. Maybe it was a garbage dump. What was strange besides their numbers was their silence. They might have been quarrelling and nagging, as crows do, but we couldn't hear through the thick glass of the windows. The silence made their flight seem prophetic, loaded with some meaning we couldn't grasp. Patrick writes in his memoir that the paths of birds "are known only to themselves, though if you watch them closely you can see them following invisible pathways through the air. Only when they are frightened do they break their patterns of travel, and that shattering of habit is more about survival than chaos. As it is in the bird world, so in ours. We break our path when fear tells us to live." These crows, steady in their journey, didn't feel this fear. It was we, watching them behind the hospital window, who did.


Shortly after we moved into our current house twelve years ago, the main gate to our front garden collapsed in the wind. Patrick designed and built another made of thin strips of wood and stalks of bamboo with a round bamboo handle few could figure out how to turn. The gate looked so organic and refined it was featured in a garden design book, but it, too, buckled in a storm—perhaps all gates get tired of standing up and swinging, and want to fall face-down to the earth. Without the energy needed to build a new one and with his faith in his carpentry skills starting to fray, early this year he hired a boat builder he knew to construct a new entryway between the driveway and the front garden.

Patrick and I checked out Asian designs that would match the theme of our place—our lanterns, the cherry trees twisted by age and storms into an epitome of wabi-sabi, the four *Pieris japonica* with their white spillage of blossoms and red leaves, Patrick's bonsai, our carefully chosen Columbia River stones set in the path to match our stride. What we came up with resembles a torii gate, two tall vertical posts topped by two horizontal bars curved slightly upwards. Around since the mid-Heian period in the tenth century, such gates have been used to mark the entrance to holy sites, particularly Shinto shrines. There are no such shrines in our front yard, but our gate, we decided, was worthy of the ancient torii form. It would announce the threshold between the mundanity of the gravel driveway and the enclosed garden which, in the honouring of the plants and river stones we'd carefully selected and placed, was sacred to us and, we hoped, to the animals that lived there or winged or padded through on their way to somewhere else.

All gates herald a transition: a movement from outer to inner and back again, a passage to something that needs protection from invaders, a step into a space defined as different and more valued than what is on the other side. They're an invitation but also an impediment. Signalling a need for privacy, this gate would make visitors pause, hesitate, delay, before they walked through. Some might choose to turn around and not enter the private enclosure presaged by such an imposing construction. Just as well. Something is being protected, secluded, differentiated from what's on the other side. Something is being sanctified. Is the time we have left what is being sheltered? Isn't there a holiness to our diminishing days?

The builder took his task seriously because he was a serious man but also because he admired Patrick and his writing, especially his memoir. The local lumber wasn't good enough. He started the project by driving up island to select the most noble cedar posts and cross bars, ten-foot poles he sensed wanted to find a new home in a poet's garden. They aged for months in part of a hangar he rented at the airport while he showed us draft after draft of his designs. There would be no nails; the joints would be the kind he used in boats. He and I spent over an hour selecting the precise shade of red that would run in a thin horizontal line across one of the top bars and around the circular opening at the centre.

Because Patrick didn't have the energy, I selected the hardware we had to order from a foundry in the States. As with his old gate, the mechanics to open and close the latch would end up perplexing the casual visitor and might stop some from walking through. Maybe my unconscious was at work. I wanted people to be tested, to have difficulty entering. They had to pause at the gate and, when it didn't open easily, after several clumsy efforts, come to an understanding of the only way it could possibly work: they had to lift the black, circular latch, turn it to the left, and push through. It was an elegant solution. Like the reader of a poem, they had to delve deeply and patiently into the language of the small mechanics before they would discover the workings and be let inside.

The builder's skill and precision paid off. The gate is rooted in place, looking both remarkable and natural, both old and new. It belongs here as we do. And I hope it will stay years after we have to leave. For the first few weeks in the early spring, five months after the builder began his painstaking labour, I watched Patrick mustering the strength to walk into the front yard, even when he didn't feel like getting out of bed, to stand in the middle of the posts, turn the latch, swing the gate open, walk through, and walk back out again. He hadn't felt such pleasure in a material thing, he said, since he drove his red Ford Ranger off the lot ten years ago. Whenever I pass by that brand and colour of truck going to town or coming home, my heart jumps. It's my darling, I think, and then I correct myself. It's a stranger behind the wheel of a pickup that is not Patrick's. He hasn't driven for two years.

Last November, when our friend Seán Virgo was visiting from Saskatchewan and Patrick was in the hospital, I gave him the keys for the truck and told him to use it whenever he wanted. Seán knocked on my office door and said, "Lorna, I'm so sorry. The cab of the truck is full of mould." From the look on my face, he knew I took this as a metaphor—how could I not? I hadn't started the truck every few days, I hadn't taken care of it, and now it too suffered a sickness, a grey hoarfrost coating the dashboard, door panels, steering wheel, windshield, and seats. With Seán's help and a litre of vinegar, we scrubbed it away, though you can still see lichen-like ghosts if you look closely.

After Patrick got out of the hospital in mid-May, I booked a caterer and planned a garden party. It was the year and month of my seventieth birthday, and I'd succumbed to magical thinking. If we celebrated our new gate, Patrick's tentative recovery, and my birthday, he would stay well and recover his strength. He'd made it home in time to bathe in the smell of the wisteria blooming outside of our kitchen. I reminded him of the opening of one of his poems: "You say *wisteria* and something plunders you / a mouth heavy with blue." The party would take place on May 27, three days after my actual birthday, and I invited forty-four people, all whom I cared for and whom we'd met in our thirty years on Vancouver Island. We hadn't seen most of them in months.

Illness is as isolating as alcoholism. It shuts others out, not because you don't want their love and concern but because the sick one can't survive more than a few minutes of conversation, and the caregiver is just too damned tired to meet for coffee or a glass of wine or go to a movie or concert with a friend. When I do go out to see a film or a play or attend a reading, I tend to go alone. When I'm with someone else, I don't want to talk about Patrick, saying the same thing I've been saying for months about his puzzling disease; nor do I want to talk about anything else. I'm not good to be around.

Whatever else it was going to be, this party would be a shout-out to life, however limited, with both of us still alive, but fragile, vulnerable, scared. Mortal. And we had a beautiful gate to walk through.

To get ready, we needed to get the garden looking its best. Our two gardeners, whom we'd hired a couple of years before to help with the heavy tasks when Patrick couldn't do them anymore, started pruning and rejuvenating old beds and hauling out a ton of thick clay impenetrable even by the tough engineering of earthworms. They dug in load after load of new soil. No wonder d trouble keeping plants alive in that section of the garden! My friend Kevin Paul, of the W̱SÁNEĆ Nation, is one of the few of his generation who speaks and writes in his mother tongue. Kevin told me that the area where we live—called Coles Bay on the municipal maps—is known by his people as W̱SÍ,KEM. It means "Little Place of Clay." We shouldn't be surprised by the poor drainage, the pools that gather in the front yard after a heavy rain or the way the soil cracks like a turtle's moulting shell after only a week of dryness.

The party gave me a sense of purpose. I weeded in a frenzy, planted, filled in the bald spots on our pathways with shovelfuls of gravel, edged the lawns with a special spade, prowled the nurseries for quick fixes—blooming annuals I could plunk into empty spaces. Patrick wanted to finish the fence on the side of the gate— the task he'd started but had to abandon—but he knew he couldn't do it in a week. His son Michael came to help. Patrick leaned against the sawhorse, standing upright, cutting the planks and passing them to Michael, who bent over and nailed them in place. It took less than an hour and the fence was done. "This used to be nothing," Patrick said. "Now I can't do it on my own." I reminded him he'd had pneumonia, he'd lain immobile for two weeks, and his muscles had atrophied.

One doctor told us that once you're eighty, for every day in bed it takes seven to recover. Just from this latest setback, not counting the pneumonia, it would take over three months for his strength to return. "Be patient," I said, running my hand over his high forehead. "You'll be okay." I longed for that to be true. It had become impossible for us to discern the difference between slow healing and a steady, implacable decline. Whatever in our bodies is the source of hope was wearing thin as the wings of a moth—though the moth was still thudding into the porch light.

We had the party. It was a warm, late-spring day, and everyone strolled or glided around the garden, many of the women in colourful dresses and sun hats as if part of an English country revival. The caterer's two staff swirled up and down the paths, trays of appetizers balanced in their hands. It was the first time we'd ever hired someone to cook and serve and clean up afterward. Patrick sat in the gazebo, and I buzzed by to see who he was talking to and if he was okay, then buzzed out again. I've stored snapshots in my mind of clusters of friends in various places in the garden, some on the bench under the bamboo, a knot of them near the raspberry patch in the far back, several in a line along the pond, but I remember few conversations. I had fallen into a trance.

Throughout the afternoon, I flitted in a blur from one person to the next, pausing for a chat but not really engaging, because the purpose of this party was not for me to visit or reconnect but to stir up all good will and energy and aim it at Patrick so he would heal. It was the bargain I had made with my passel of holy charms: the splendid gate, the ivy-free trees in the park, my birthday, his coming home from his sick bed, Basho's continued presence among us. In a maddened state, I tossed back glass after glass of celebratory wine. It sloshed through my body and my brain and washed away the worry along with any detailed scenes that might have settled as memories, any words I might have said. When I bent over the large birthday cake to blow out the candles, my silver pendant, a gift from Patrick, swung through the icing and swung back, smudging the front of my linen dress, my face and chin, with a thick white sweetness. In the pictures I look like a messy little kid, grinning insanely.

———

I think back to Patrick's patience in taming Po Chu and wish he could train that same persistent fortitude and faith on himself. Just as she is becoming more trusting and calmer, he could grow stronger. Much to our surprise, and maybe to Po's, she's become a beautiful cat. I imagine her being startled when she glimpses herself in the glassy surface of the pond. Who is this stunning creature! Her coat is thick and satiny to the touch, her tail could win a prize for plushness, her whiskers and eyebrows gleam long and black in the sun. Under and on both sides of her coal-smudged face streaked with orange flares a thick, luxurious muff wider than an Elizabethan collar. We continue to be students of her body language, knowing when it's safe to pet her and when it isn't—she still lashes out— but she seeks our company and cuddles my bathrobe if I leave it on the bed. Patrick had warned, "Don't expect her to be an affectionate cat. That's not who she is." But it's who, with his care, she's turning out to be.

After the party, Patrick had two blissful weeks at home. His breathing wasn't shallow; his lungs must have been healing. I was scheduled to go away again, this time to Wintergreen Studios for four days in June, including two days of travel. It's a big lodge built out of straw bales and hunkered on a treed swatch of land outside of Kingston. Rena Upitis, the woman who built it, envisioned a centre of the arts, ecology, and learning. After seven years, that's exactly what it's become. She was waiting for me there with two photographers whom I'd teamed up with to work on a book, pictures they'd taken at Wintergreen paired with my poems. Our model was *The Wild in You*, a collaboration between me and the environmental activist and photographer Ian McAllister. The title of the new book would end up being *The House the Spirit Builds*.

At this rural retreat, what a creative time we had, they lining up prints of the photos on three long tables, me twinning them with pages of poetry. The photographers, Rena, and I swooped in and out trying other pairings, changing the order, yelping with delight when we found the perfect match. It had been a long time since creativity had been central to my life. One of the poems sprang from an intriguing photo of a broken salt shaker made of white china and shaped like a small chef. You turned it upside down to shake it, holes punched in the top of the tall hat; but now, the head broken, salt had spilled like a soft sigh of snow on the tablecloth. Though I wrote the lines several months ago, thinking they were simply about the image in the photograph, I was shocked when I revisited the poem as we pulled the book together: how much the words said about what I was feeling now. I'd forgotten the prescient nature of poems, their seer-like ability to speak things even the poet won't admit to herself in the process of creation.

BREAKAGE

At 3 a.m. a shattering and you fear
something inside you has broken.


When you walk into the kitchen hours later
you see the salt shaker's
busted (was a pin pulled from the top?), crystals exploding


on the table—a spill of damage and bad luck.
Someone has carried off most of it.
If the grains had been sweet, you'd arrest the ants.


You toss what's left over one shoulder, then the other,
not remembering which side's the curse, which the cure.
No one sees you are not the same: no one sees

you've been ruined. Salt in a wound
helps the healing: that's another saying
you should heed. Did the moon last night

slide its bovine tongue across the table, across the part of you
that's damaged? O, how the moon longs
for the ocean, how it loves the taste of salt

on anyone's hurt skin.

When I flew home, Patrick again wasn't at the airport to meet me, but at least this time he wasn't in emergency—he was at the house, unable to drive. His right foot looked like an elephant's, grey and swollen, his hand the size of a catcher's mitt. And once more he'd sunk into deep fatigue, sleeping eighteen hours a day. Two days previously, at an already-scheduled appointment his brother drove him to, the rheumatologist had diagnosed gout. *Gout?* I'd mistakenly attributed that disease to an overly rich diet, like Henry VIII's, but I discovered online that it's connected to rheumatoid arthritis. Patrick was scheduled for an X-ray to see if any indicative crystals sparkled beneath his skin like frost quilling blades of grass.

The next morning, he insisted on clipping unwanted poplar saplings along our back fence. Clumsy on his big foot, he fell on the gravel path. I came upon him in the house standing by the laundry sink next to the washing machine, blood spotting the tiled floor and leaving a trail where he'd walked from the kitchen door down the long hall to the back room. I tried not to panic—he's on blood thinners and the splatter or spill from any scoring of his skin makes the injury look worse than what it is. Dabbing at the scrapes and gashes with pieces of paper towel, he said he was sure he'd cracked some ribs.

That afternoon I called a friend whose husband, coincidentally, was also on blood thinners. He too had cut himself while pruning in the garden and had bled all over the wool rug by the kitchen sink as he tried to staunch the flow. "Will we have to throw out the rug?" he'd asked her. "John," she said, "I know how to get blood out of fabric. I've spent years doing it." I suggested that if it had been a woman who'd injured herself, she'd have bled in one compact spot. She wouldn't leave a pathway of gore from the back door to the sink. We both laughed and it felt good, this unabashed, guilt-free laughter not snuffed out by sadness and worry.

June, 2018

JUST AFTER THE SUMMER SOLSTICE Patrick and I gather at the house of Richard, Patrick's youngest son, for his forty-first birthday. He and his wife have three kids under ten. Richard's older brother Michael, his wife, and their three children are there as well. Patrick sits alone on the couch, the rest of the adults perched at the kitchen counter, and the grandkids come to him in dribs and drabs in between the games they're playing. I let him be. The grandkids are fascinated by his swollen monster hand and the blotchy, purple-black bruises that ladder up both arms. Usually he wears long sleeves like a secret heroin addict because he's embarrassed by this dark patchwork of age and disease. I remember my own grandfather, his skin so thin and easily blackened. As a kid, I didn't know what it meant. Both sons and their wives take turns sitting beside Patrick for a while, quietly talking. It's as if the habits from the hospital visits are impossible to break.

We're tired when we get home, but that isn't unusual. After an hour of TV we climb into bed. Moaning when he rolls over, almost panting, Patrick says, "Don't worry. It's just my ribs." Around two a.m. he wakes me. "You have to help me out of bed to the bathroom. I can't get up." I run around to his side and pull him to his feet. Though he's lost over forty pounds, he feels like a sack of stones. "I'm calling an ambulance," I say.

"No, you're not calling an ambulance."

Out of bed, he pushes me away when I try to hold him up, and hobbles to the toilet. "I'm not going to the hospital." I sit in the dark on the edge of the mattress and listen to the sound of urine hitting the water in the bowl. Back in bed, panting again, he starts shaking. "You're not calling anyone. It's the weekend." He rolls onto his side with a moan. "I'm okay."

*Not again, not again*, I repeat to myself. When do I listen to him and when do I dial emergency? What is respect for his wishes versus stupidity on my part? He's panting like an animal in distress. It can't be just his cracked ribs, can it? In the dark I hurry from our room to the kitchen and phone 911. I respond to the operator's questions, my voice catching in my throat like a wad of cotton. Back in the bedroom, I tell him I made the call and turn on the lights outside our bedroom's sliding glass doors and in the carport so the ambulance driver can locate the house. There are no street-lights. Our road and driveway are dark. Sitting on the edge of the bed again, he can't get up. "Help me," he says.

Basho, at eighteen, like Patrick has trouble balancing; some days he seems less than a shadow, merely skin and bones and a matted coat that he's stopped grooming. I don't know how he leaps up the four levels of the high tower to exit through the elevated bedroom window that functions as our cat door, but he does. And he loves to lie on the top shelf lording it over Po Chu, whom he won't let up. Every morning before he sniffs at his breakfast, he goes on his walkabout down the garden path, through the archway to the far end of the property, and then he comes back through the archway again and strolls diagonally across the moss to the pond. He stops at the top where the waterfall begins its sputter and he steps, oh so carefully, on the rocks humped only slightly above the water. A low stone bridge with gaps. His paws stay dry as he pads across.

I don't why it's important to him to drink on the far side of the upper pool rather than the closer one, but as he drops his head and hunches his shoulders, for a moment and from a distance, he's a young, feral animal, coming from the shadows to satisfy his thirst. I watch him from the kitchen window as if I'm sitting in a hide, surprised by what creatures appear at the watering hole in the early morning. After his careful wobbly walk back to the house, on the cement pad in front of our library door he collapses in the sun, looking like a tossed-away, dusty rag someone found in the back of a shed and wiped their hands on. When I'm near him, I shoo away the fly that tries to settle on his head.

He's completely deaf and, without the benefit of hearing aids, even if I pound my feet heavily on the wood floor or the deck so he knows I'm coming, I startle him. I let him know I'm there by touch, bending to stroke the top of his head where his markings are so beautiful. Every day, I tell myself, may be his last. Yesterday was particularly bad. He ate only a tablespoon of food and swayed on his skinny legs when he stood like a badly built fence buffeted by wind.

I keep trying to coach myself to be ready to say goodbye, but there's no way for sorrow to be rehearsed and made less devastating. No foreknowledge can help or shorten its span. On researching the names of knots for a poem I'm writing, I come across two that say it all: blood knot and grief knot. Surely they're tied together inside the body whenever you attach yourself to someone, animal or human. Maybe they're intertwined in the umbilical cord in the piece below the cut. Maybe that's why you see those who are grief-stricken double over and clutch their bellies, because that's where the pain begins and where it goes home to.

From HE'S ONLY A CAT

I've been crying for a week
over the cat. There are some
I can say this to and others
I cannot. *He's only a cat,*
many reply. I now divide
people into these two camps.
It's one way of knowing the world.

The other illness that nearly destroyed Patrick, and me along with him, was alcoholism. When his drinking became more important than anything else, about fifteen years into our lives together, I began to write him letters though we lived in the same house and the studies where we worked were side by side. Talking to him wasn't doing any good. He wasn't hearing my angst, my despair, the devastating feeling that I'd have to go or ask him to leave. Besides, I'd always end up crying and the conversation (was it ever a conversation?) would blubber to a stop. My recurring theme was that if he loved me enough he'd stop drinking. Wasn't that what it was all about? Love. That's the plea I kept returning to in the letters I'd leave on his desk in the morning. I had, even in my late forties, the naïve belief that love could cure anything. How could I have lived that long and held onto such a simple, happy-ever-after equation like some little girl playing with princess dolls, like some heroine in a sappy romance?

A few months of twice-a-week Al-Anon meetings convinced me there was nothing I could do to drag him out of drunkenness and into sobriety. The pull of addiction was stronger than any feelings for anyone—a child, a spouse, a parent; it was stronger than honesty, integrity, self-respect. Stronger than the need to pay the bills, stay out of jail, stay married, stay cogent, stay on the road, stay alive. If he was going to stop, he had to do it for himself, not for me. He had to have his own reason. Something inside him had to become fierce enough to climb above the roar of addiction deep in his belly, and survive.

Once, in the middle of the night, I looked up to see him standing at the end of our bed, silhouetted in the light from the bathroom. As much to himself as to me, he said, "You know, if I have to choose—if I have to choose between being sober and being a poet, I'll choose to be sober." I was stunned. What a Faustian cost; the genius of his writing was surely equivalent to the value of a soul. His addiction was killing him, he couldn't be a whole person if he continued drinking, yet he'd written all of his books with a bottle and a pack of cigarettes on his desk. Booze was his inspiration; it swung open the gate to poetry's truths and insights, its linguistic dazzle and daring.

Patrick got sober, he told me months later, because he decided to live. I don't know what it was that tilted him toward death and then away from it, but I do remember the morning he left for treatment. His sponsor, a stocky female probation officer dressed in an aqua sweatshirt and matching pull-on pants, met him at our front door where he waited with a small suitcase. He'd be gone for at least six weeks, resident at a rehabilitation centre about two hours away on the outskirts of Nanaimo. I had to get a loan from our bank to pay the fees. I choked through a short goodbye, not knowing if he'd dry out, if he'd want to come home at the end of his stay, or who he'd be if he did. His sponsor gave me a big hug and said, "Honey, things are going to get better." Then, after Patrick slid into the passenger side of her car, she returned to the step where I was standing and added, "I'll be back if that's okay with you. To check the house for bottles."

"He told me he threw them out," I said. I'd believed him.

"I'll be back this afternoon." There was no messing around with her. Thank God Patrick was in her hands.

Before I'd learned my Al-Anon lessons—among them, that I couldn't control his drinking—some nights after he'd gone to bed, I searched the yard and house for booze. He'd sworn that he'd quit, but all my antennae were quivering. Over the years he'd substituted brandy and port for scotch, his favourite, thinking because he liked them less, he wouldn't drink as much. A friend of ours did the same with gin, exchanging it for his favourite spirit, screech, but he died of drinking just the same. Finally Patrick ended up with vodka because its smell on his breath was harder to detect. I'd find the empties and half-filled bottles behind the books on his shelves, under the towels in the linen cupboard, stacked between chunks of firewood in the woodpile, under the seat in his truck, and tucked in the ivy that climbed the outdoor chimney. My moments of triumph were short-lived. *Aha!* I'd say to myself in the dark of the garden, clad only in my red flannel nightgown. I'd sit on the step with the proof in my hands and not know what to do, what to say to him in the morning. It had all been said before.

As his sponsor got behind the wheel, I heard her say, "I hope you peed. We're not stopping till we hit the treatment centre." There was no way she was going to allow him to be alone, even for a few minutes in a gas-station men's room. Who knew where he could have hidden a bottle? He'd tricked me endless times tucking a flat mickey under his sweater in the small of his back, the belt on his jeans holding it tight, as we headed off for an evening together. Even if I hugged him, which I often did, I couldn't feel it.

Patrick's brilliant memoir, *There Is a Season,* about his road to recovery, included his weeks in treatment, but before he started writing it, we co-edited an anthology about addiction. We didn't send out a call for essays; instead we asked authors whom we admired, many of them friends, if they'd create a non-fiction piece about their battles with alcohol or cigarettes or heroin. Those close to them knew about their substance abuse but it wasn't public knowledge. Some of them were clean and sober, others not. A few turned us down, but the ten writers who agreed included David Adams Richards, Peter Gzowski, Stephen Reid, and Marnie Woodrow. We thought we needed to match their courage with our own, so Patrick and I wrote essays too, him about his drinking days and me about my struggles with them.

It was a difficult place for both of us to revisit, but even more difficult was talking about the book once it was published. It's funny, but when you're the kind of writers we are, in the midst of trying to find one word after another, figuring out what it is you feel about things and what you want to say, searching for the best words in the best order, you don't think about who's going to read your work or who's going to want to talk to you about it after it hits the market. Though we'd both done the obligatory tour for dozens of books, this time it felt different. This time, talking about our years and days enmeshed in Patrick's addiction, we felt stripped to the bones. Those upset about how we'd exposed ourselves in *No Longer Two People* might have felt a similar discomfort if they'd heard us read in public from this book, twenty-two years later.

In spite of our hesitation, our publisher had no trouble finding people who wanted to talk to us. We were interviewed by June Callwood on stage to a sold-out crowd at the International Festival of Authors in Toronto; for CTV we engaged in a live and lengthy conversation with Pamela Wallin, who with her typical bluntness asked Patrick how he could have put me through this and asked me how I could have stayed; on CBC Radio's *Sounds Like Canada* the new host, Shelagh Rogers, spoke with us, Marnie Woodrow, and Peter Gzowski, hooked up to an oxygen tank and in the last stages of emphysema. Though he could have written about alcoholism along with most of the others in the book, his essay dealt with smoking. It was amusing to hear him trying to wrestle the microphone from Shelagh, falling back into his old role of asking the questions instead of answering them. Peter teased Patrick and me about getting married only a couple of weeks before, and neither of us remembering the exact date. "Who just gets married and already forgets the date?" A couple who'd been living together for twenty-three years, I guess.

That hour with Shelagh rippled across the country. Patrick's voice broke when he talked of living with a need that ate him from the inside out every hour of the day, and it broke again when he listed the names of fellow writers and friends who'd died from alcohol's grip: Alden Nowlan, Gwendolyn MacEwan, Milton Acorn, Al Pittman. He also talked about his gratitude for me, how supportive and loving I had been. I can't remember if I corrected him on air: I didn't deserve anyone's gratitude or praise. It wasn't love or loyalty that had kept me with him. It was my own weakness—who would I be without him; could I make it on my own?—and it was my childhood. Living with alcoholism and its chaos was what I had known in my mother's and father's house. It was what I felt comfortable with. Now that he was sober I was grateful that I'd stayed and that he'd embarked on a new and temperate life. But if I'd been a healthy person, I wouldn't have stuck around.

A week after his sponsor dropped him off at the treatment centre, she asked me to meet her for coffee. She'd just come from work at the probation office and was dressed in a navy blue suit-jacket with matching pants. The conservative look was challenged by her hair, the yellow of a crossing guard's vest. I waited for her to start the conversation. She leaned toward me across the booth and clutched both my hands. There was no escaping her. "Why do you think so little of yourself?" she asked. "Why are you not get-ting hold of your life?" I had expected sympathy from her, perhaps admiration for my perseverance, my weepy support of my partner. Not a challenge that left me shaken.

A KIND OF LOVE

You can see it
in my graduation photograph.
You're Daddy's little girl, he said,
his arm heavy around my shoulders,
his face too naked, a sloppy
smile sliding to one side.
I held him up. Mom tied his shoes.
His love made me ashamed.

Some days I felt protective,
his hangdog look at breakfast
when no one talked to him but me,
sugar spilling from his spoon.
Don't tell Mum, he'd say

on Sundays when he took me boating,
sunk his third empty in the lake.
At home she fried a chicken
in case he didn't catch a fish,
waited and kept things warm.
Even so, he died too soon.

Now I wait for you as if
you've spent a summer afternoon
in waves of wind and sunlight. I know
you've hidden a bottle somewhere
upstairs in your room. So far
I've stopped myself from looking
though I can't find what to do.

More and more I'm Daddy's
little girl in peau de soi,
my first long dress, its false
sheen a wash of blue.
When you lean into me
the same look's on your face
as in the photograph.
Your smile's undone.

Among the other things
it could be named
this too is love, the kind
I'm most familiar with—
the weight I claim
I cannot bear, and do,
and do.

TVOntario's *Imprint* won the prize for the most taxing interview in the most inappropriate location. We met the host on the second floor of a bar off Bloor Street at eleven in the morning. This was the usual setting for the literary segment of the program. It was early enough not to be noisy, and it looked hip, I guess, but the bartender, when she heard what the book was about, said, with no humour in her voice, "There go my tips." Although she'd just started her shift, she looked every one of her forty-odd years in the room's unforgiving mirrors behind the shelves of bottles flashier than Christmas lights. I worried about Patrick's new sobriety. Would the strobe of liquid colours shine too tempting a brightness on his newfound serenity and make him want a shot? Would he topple from his weeks of recovery?

After talking to me briefly, the host queried Patrick about his reasons for co-editing the book. Patrick talked openly about his dark nights of the soul when the hours revolved around one thing only—to get enough booze into his system to function, yet keep his drinking hidden. It was hell, he said, and it took up all his energy. As he told his story, I glanced at the two men slumped on stools down the bar from him. They leaned on their elbows, side by side, but they weren't talking; their heads were turned toward Patrick. Both of them had the look of regulars, hovering over their drinks and blurred around the edges.

When Patrick talked about how his drunkenness had wrecked two families, the bartender left the glasses she was drying and walked to the shadows at the back of the room, her face to the wall, her shoulders shuddering. As she dabbed at her eyes with her apron, one of the men shuffled over and put his arm around her. I wondered what her story was and what part of Patrick's had connected with her so deeply. Did she love someone whose drinking was out of control? Was she struggling with demons herself?

At the end of the interview, as the camera crew packed up, the other habitué of the bar slid off his stool and walked over to where we sat. Swaying a little as if the floor was a raft tossed by rapids, he leaned into Patrick. He'd been sober till he started drinking again three days ago, he said. Now out of the blue look what's appeared in his pub—a camera crew, a TV show, and a guardian angel who would help him stop. Patrick led him to a table in the back and sat with him, talking quietly. The man sipped a beer. This indeed might have been the moment that changed that man's life. Or his desire to quit might have lasted only as long as it took us to walk down the stairs and leave the bar for our next interview.

Our next interview? This was our last. Patrick phoned the press and told them to cancel the others they'd set up. After David Adams Richards read with us at Harbourfront that night, he walked off the stage and stopped by our chairs. "I love you guys," he said, "and I don't regret writing this. But I won't read it or talk about it again." We got it. The anthology's now in its third printing, expanded to include addictions like gaming that weren't in the first edition. Responses that have come our way affirm the book has done some good, and the words are there for anyone to read. But, like David, at a certain point we'd had enough of public heartache.

When we got back home, feeling frail and spent, there was a letter waiting. It was from a well-known Toronto visual artist who'd heard the CBC program while he was driving to his lakeside cottage with three twenty-sixes of vodka stashed in his backpack. He had a show in a gallery coming up and he'd told his girlfriend he wanted to be alone so he could paint. The truth was he wanted to be alone so he could drink. Patrick's words on the radio, he wrote, made him swerve the car to the shoulder and toss the vodka in the ditch. The more environmentally correct option—open the bottles, pour the liquid out, and recycle—wasn't a choice. The smell of the alcohol would have been too much for him to resist. The bottles glinting in the grass, he wrenched the car around and drove back to the city. When we met him at his studio on Front Street in Toronto a few months later, he was sober.

## September, 2018

BASHO HAS TAKEN to yowling when he comes in from outside or when he walks down the long hallway. I don't know if the heart-piercing sound means he's in pain or just confused. Is he looking for something? Is he yowling so loudly because he can't hear himself and isn't aware of the noise he's making? Along with his joints petrifying into stiffness, all his heightened tiger senses have been kidnapped. It must be wretched for him not to hear the singing of the yellow warblers that dip in the pond, the splash of the turtles as they clatter from the rocks into the water, the sharp metallic sound of a can opening. And his once-bright eyes are clouded. Instead of holding the blue of a high mountain lake, they look swampy. I don't know what he sees.

Normally, in late afternoon, when the sun slants through Patrick's office window, Basho stretches out in a warm patch on the rug by the desk where Patrick works. They've been daily companions our twelve years in this house. Basho's calm presence has been part of the silence between the lines in Patrick's poems, part of the animal spirit that comes alive in his writing, circling and lying down in the white space in the margins of the page. The room's been empty for a week now with Patrick back in the hospital—the third stint this year—and, with him gone, Basho's found another place to nap, usually on the top of the couch in the library where the electric heater blasts hot air up the wall. But one afternoon, when I look all over the house and can't find him to badger him to eat, I glance inside the doorway of Patrick's office, where Basho hasn't been for days. There he is, lying in his usual swatch of sunlight by the desk. When I call him and rattle his bag of treats, he doesn't move. I step inside and walk closer. There's a mouse between his front paws. How on his rickety legs, deaf and almost blind, did he catch a mouse? Did it run into him and die of shock?

I feel so proud of my once-brilliant hunter who regularly brought home mice, rats, and rabbits, whom he beheaded on the hall rug where they bled out like something in a horror film. I had to clean up the stains and pick up the little that was left: a tail, a hind rabbit leg, a bile duct perfectly preserved. This mouse, though lifeless, is intact, unchewed, wet with spit. His prey's wholeness, its integrity, is unusual for him. Surely it's a blessing, a small offering for his friend who's been so long away. Basho, too, wants Patrick to come home.


"Yes, dear." Those two words, endemic to a long marriage, sound agreeable, meek, insipid, but to my ear, they reek of exasperation and disdain. What the spouse really wants to say is, *Bugger off.* Did you take your pills? Yes, dear. Did you clean your hearing aids? Yes, dear. Don't forget to eat a banana. Yes, dear. It's a signal that I have to stop. Stop reminding, stop nagging, stop controlling. I don't want to be this person, sister to Nurse Ratched—kinder, yes, but a sharp-eyed vigilante of my husband's health. I can feel myself sinking into crankiness and impatience. I am not a woman who laughs, who snuggles, who dances, who jokes, who flares into anger without guilt. I am a woman who lives with a man who has become a patient, a worry, a passive shuffler from mattress to couch, a moaner, a shaker, a bleeder. How do either of us break out of this? How do we become the companions, lovers, artists on the edge we once were? Is that all gone for good?

In my bleaker moments, I can't help but wonder if Patrick's illness is our just dessert, arriving late to the table but arriving nevertheless, the waiter having chosen this final course when he saw us enter the room. When Patrick asked me to leave my marriage (as he would leave his) and travel with him, I felt no compunction. I hurled myself and all my longing into what I knew would be an artistic life with a man who was mad, taboo-breaking, out-of-the-fucking-ordinary. I wanted him, I wanted the craziness of what we'd create together. Even if we didn't last, I didn't care who got hurt.

We smashed everything to hurl ourselves into our new life. He left his wife and two little kids. I shattered my ten-year marriage, my teaching job, my master's thesis, the good opinion of my friends and family—everything destroyed for the sake of being with this man. I knew there'd be storms, drunkenness, fights, harm; but I, a person normally full of fear, didn't worry about the cost. I'd never before done anything so destructive and daring, so without concern for what other people thought or for the damage done. This is not admirable or blameworthy, it's just the way it was. And I don't regret it.

LOVE SONG

Hair has a mind
of its own. At night

it lifts from your pillow
and mates with the wind.
That is why it is so knotted
and tangled in the morning,
why it breaks the teeth
of your finest combs,
spills from ribbons and barrettes.

It has spent
the night with the wind.
Can't you feel its wantonness
as it falls across your shoulders?

Did I become a different person or had my former self been loosely stitched from practical, but flimsy, cloth? A warp and weave of tougher, glitzy threads lay beneath the outer surface, waiting to be pulled and woven into a flashy jacket I'd wear when we met. Our love affair, without the calming effects of children, religious sensibilities, the need for public approbation, was built on poetry and lust. Who knew there'd be time or space for domestic complacency, addiction, a devastating illness, a durable abiding respect and affection, the common banality of a man and woman living together year after year after year, a garden, a house, a cat and a cat and a cat.

In her novel *The Waterfall*, Margaret Drabble, describing a couple in the throes of an unexpectedly long extramarital affair, writes, "It isn't artistic to linger on like this." One of us should have had a spectacular fling that drove the other out the door; we should have wounded each other—as we did, but in a place that wouldn't heal. We should have burst into flames side by side in an accident. Oh, there were betrayals, there were fights, there were wine glasses thrown against the wall and drunken driving, the front wheels drifting over the yellow line, Patrick steering with one hand over his eye because he was seeing double, me scared and angry but going with him, not shouting for him to pull over, to drop me off.

I want this car of illness and worry to stop. I want to yank open the door and leap out. No, to be more accurate: I want to sit beside him in the passenger seat of forty years ago, he behind the wheel, singing every Dylan song he knew, my head on his shoulder, my hand on his thigh, the sun burning up the road behind as we rolled down the long line of blacktop that crosses the plains, landing at last on the shores of Lake Winnipeg where we sat where the waves licked the sand and wrote letters home telling our spouses we weren't coming back. It was a cowardly way to end our marriages, but I didn't care. I was doing what I wanted to do. I was throwing myself into an idiot wind and it was blowing me away.

Poetry: that's been how I've defined myself for close to fifty years; it's how I've made sense of things, how I've made my living—well, that combined with teaching—and, equally as important, how I've made my way through the world. Line by line, heartbeat by heartbeat. It's who I am, who Patrick is, it's how we met.

In 1976, I was still teaching high school and working as a guidance counsellor in Swift Current. I'd left my husband once, but ended up returning after four months. A year after patching up my marriage, I was alone in my car on the way to Regina, three hours away, for a day-long workshop at the library—led by Patrick Lane. One of my poetry friends from Moose Jaw, Robert Currie, had given me Patrick's *Beware the Months of Fire*. He said, "I think you'd really like this guy." He meant the poetry.

In the black-and-white author photo on the back of the book, Patrick hunches into a bulky winter jacket. He was so folded into himself, maybe from the cold, when the picture was taken, that he had a double chin. I'd have said he was fat and old (meaning over fifty; I was twenty-eight.") I can swear with honesty that I was driving three hours to work with him not because of any attraction to the man but because of the lure of the poems. Lines like "The bird you captured is dead. / I told you it would die / but you would not learn / from my telling. You wanted / to cage a bird in your hands / and learn to fly." Lines like "He doesn't remember where / he met her or why he is still / with her. He has been watching / two vultures fight over the body / of a rat and he has made a bet / with the fat man who owns the bar / that the bird with one leg will win." The terrible beauty Yeats wrote about sounded in these words, such honesty, such hard-won truth, such blood and salt and brokenness. I'd heard nothing like them before, and I wanted to hear them again from the mouth of the man who'd made them. I wanted to know how to write so brilliantly, so coldly, so fearlessly. I wanted to taste it.

Six of my friends were at the workshop—Robert Currie, Gary Hyland, Judy Krause, Byrna Barclay, Ted Dyck, and Jim McLean—part of a group I met with once a month in Moose Jaw to work on our poems. I'd leave Swift Current on a Friday night when school was out and hit the road with a case of beer and three poems in my back pocket. They were my pals, my mentors, my audience, people to write toward, peers who made me feel my poetry mattered to someone, anyone, besides me. It was Robert's idea to invite Patrick, who lived and worked in a small town on B.C.'s Sunshine Coast and who, Robert had been told, could use the money. The Saskatchewan Arts Board provided a small grant to bring him in.

When I walked into the room where everyone had gathered, I tried not to stare at the man sitting at the head of the table. He wasn't old, he had only ten or so years on me, and he wasn't fat. He was lean and fit—later he told us he'd been working all summer building houses. That was how he paid the mortgage, he said, and supported his wife and two kids. He mentioned them more than once: he didn't pretend he was available or on his own. He wore jeans and a cowboy shirt with snap buttons. I was shocked at my desire to run my fingers up his shirt and make the buttons pop. What was going on? Who did I think I was?

There was his poetry, of course, but I liked everything about him. His high forehead, the way his blond hair curled at the nape of his neck, the quickness of his blue eyes that skimmed the room as naturally as a pair of dragonflies across a pond, lighting on one person, then the next, leaving no one out. I liked how he respected us, though no one brought a poem that measured up to his, how he bit his lower lip when he was thinking about what to say about someone's lines, how he told us again and again to believe in ourselves and our stories, how he laughed easily and often but then leaned in and burned a hole through our pages with brilliant, rapt attention. I liked how he moved his raised finger to the beat of a poem, as if he were a conductor. I liked his moustache, which he pulled with his thumb and index finger as he paused in his speaking.

And then there were his hands. As they gestured, as they jabbed the air to make a point—rough and tanned, large-knuckled and barked from hammering nails into boards and shingling roofs. How could I not imagine them on my skin? Oh, no. Did he catch me out? Patrick told me later he noticed my stare and, whenever the opportunity arose, he'd slap his hand on the table and rest it there. Two fingers on the right were stained with nicotine. In my blue-jean jumpsuit, I leaned forward into the force of his attention, listening to his words like someone starved of language who had just learned to read. A week after, a note addressed to me arrived at the high school where I was teaching. How did he find my address? He said he regretted we hadn't spent the night together. He said he wished he'd undone the chest-to-navel zipper on my jumpsuit. I thought, how arrogant! What made him think he had a chance? But I was thrilled, really, I was pleased. He said we'd meet again. He was right, but it wouldn't happen for two more years.

The most significant part of our first meeting took place hours after the workshop ended. The group had gone to dinner; Patrick had given a reading where I'd introduced him, quoting some of his lines by heart, then we'd gathered at Geoff Ursell's to hear CBC Radio's *Anthology* broadcast across the country, from Newfoundland to the far north to Vancouver Island. A writer and a university professor, Geoff had organized and hosted a program featuring Saskatchewan writing. About a dozen of us sat on his couches and straight-backed chairs, leaning in to listen as if we'd been transported backwards into the Golden Age of Radio when families gathered around their RCAs and Zeniths, the inner tubes drawing like magnets the graphite of words riding the airwaves. The broadcast was a big deal in 1976, a kind of coming of age for Saskatchewan poetry, a reaching out to a larger audience from coast to coast to coast. For me and several others in the room it was our national debut.

Patrick sat across from me, beer in hand, a young woman from the workshop sitting on the floor in front of him, her arms draped across his knees. Her name was Candy. No kidding. He told me later he was watching me, my head lowered as the radio voice read my poems. I looked shy and proud, he said. During a poem by Terrence Heath, who wasn't there that night, our eyes met, and something shifted inside me. *If I kept a journal, I'd say: / Today she was beautiful.* I looked up at the man who would be my only love, though I didn't know it then. *And if I kept a diary, I'd say: / Today I was beautiful.*

It was those words that reached like invisible needles threaded with catgut across the room, across our histories, our troubles, our differences, and stitched our lives together. Blood knot. Grief knot. Did I ever tell Terrence, who now lives in Toronto and who, in his decades of publishing, has concentrated mainly on art criticism, not poetry? Would he care? Have I made too much of this?

When I ask Patrick for his take, he says he doesn't recall the lines but does remember my eyes catching his, both of us compelled to look at one another because of the words streaming from the radio into the crowded living room in Regina and that singular moment of our lives. It was the look, he says, people talk about, though it sounds clichéd. "You'll find a way to write about it," he says.

## WAITING FOR A SIGN

When I met you it was as if
I was living in a house by the sea.
Waves sprayed the windows,
slapped the wooden steps.
Yet I opened the door
and a white horse stood there.
He walked through the rooms,
swinging his head from side to side,
his hooves leaving half moons
of sand on the floor.

Make what you will of this. This was
the most natural thing I've ever done,
opening the door, moving aside
for the horse to come in.

Not that you were he. He was simply
a horse, nothing more,
the gentle kind that pulls a wagon
or drags seaweed from the shore,
ankles feathered, great hooves wide as platters.

He wasn't you,
that didn't matter. He looked at me
and we knew each other. That night
I wanted to live. I wanted
to live in a house where the door
swings on hinges smooth as the sea
and a white horse stands,
waiting for a sign.

*Come in*, I said.

And that was the start of it,
the horse, the light, the electric air.
Somewhere you were walking toward me,
the door to my life swinging open,
the sea, the sea and its riderless horse
waiting to come in.

There were two more cats between our first, Nowlan, and what
may be our last, Basho and Po Chu. It's hard for me to write about
the in-betweens because they were around for too short a time,
especially the male. After Nowlan died and was buried beside the
stump of the cherry tree in the yard where Patrick set *There Is a
Season*, we contacted Al Purdy's sister-in-law, Norma, who ventured

into the most abandoned places around Victoria and picked up strays. Ironically, Al hated cats. When I suggested we might name our next one Purdy, he threatened to throw me out the door. One night Norma found a brother and sister, the rest of the litter mummified around them. For some reason the two siblings survived, the female sucking on her brother's penis as if it were a nipple. The kittens were a day or two from death. Norma bottle-fed them, named them Dickens and Roxy and, when I phoned to say we might be ready for a cat, invited us to look at them. They had to go together. We took them and we kept their names.

Dickens was a magnificent male, white with orange and black tabby swatches as if there'd been a can of paint with that mix of colour and someone had splashed him with a brush, on his back, the top of his head, his narrow hips. He was long and lithe, and he tolerated his sister curling up with him on the blue chair in front of the book shelves. Two years after he joined us, he was run over in our street. Roxy was either white with black spots or black with white. In any case, she was a spotted cat. Her legs were white, movie-star long and slim, with almost-spots on the top of her paws. She could have been vain, but she was the sweetest cat I've ever met.

Though she struggled in your arms and refused to be held or picked up, there wasn't a bad bone in Roxy's feline body. Unlike Po Chu, she never bit or scratched. Always alert, her eyes dashed from one flit of motion to another. Outside, she'd glance to the left, and I'd home in on a warbler wagging the wisteria leaves. She'd snap her head to the right and up, and I'd glimpse a raccoon nibbling cherries in the fruit-heavy boughs. All quickness and startle and gentleness was she. A master hunter who never killed a bird, she'd leap in the air at the shores of the pond and catch a dragonfly between her front paws. We'd find them in the house, clicking against the window, undamaged. As gently as we could, cupping our palms around them, we'd trap them in our hands and set them free. Even their fragile wings weren't torn.

Half asleep one spring night, darkness draped over the house, we heard a tree frog, startlingly close. We got out of bed, slid open the screen door to the front deck and looked outside, where Virginia creeper climbed the trellis near the steps. It was a favourite haunt of frogs. Nothing. The tree frog croaked again. Could it be behind the coal shuttle near the fireplace? There it was. Patrick scooped it up, carried it outside and set it among the leaves where he thought it had come from. How did it get inside? Had we left a door or window open?

A night or so later, we heard a frog again. It fell quiet, but it had been close, obviously inside the house. What was going on? We started searching—under the sideboard, behind the armchair and the coal shuttle, on the bottom bookshelf—then we glanced at Roxy, sitting beside the couch with an intense expression on her small, alert face. She looked at us, opened her mouth, and a frog jumped out. I palmed it before she could catch it again and carried it outside. What a journey for this frog! What a tale it had to tell, carried in a cat's mouth, on her tongue and between her teeth, without a mark left upon it. Without a puncture on its smooth, green skin. After she spat it out, she spat again as if its taste had not been to her liking.

Roxy lived with us for fourteen years, twelve of them with Basho. Then she, who had loved to eat, stopped eating. We cooked every delicacy, from fresh chicken livers to slices of beef to salmon and tuna, but she turned her head away. It's devastating when an animal avoids every delicacy you pass under its nose. Now I think of the two elderly daughters in the hospital across the room from me and Patrick, trying to feed their father, talking to him in voices they'd probably used decades ago on their own fussy children: "Just try a spoonful, just a taste."

Roxy died when I was away for a week teaching in Colorado. I told Patrick not to wait for me to come home when the vet couldn't get any nutrition in her except intravenously. Patrick buried her in the front garden under a low bench he'd fashioned from a slate slab. She and I had sat there in the evenings before bed, she on my lap as long as it had been her idea to be there, her soft, thin-spun hair under my hands, my eyes following hers—oh! a moth, a dragonfly, a wren in the magnolia. I sit there still. And sometimes I see what she'd see, were she beside me. Sometimes I hear a tree frog singing.

### PHOTOGRAPHER

The inventor of the shutter
and light-filter mechanism
had been watching the pupils of his cat.
Every photograph has a parallel
a cat has taken—without a touch
of sentiment, a perfect
composition of the never-seen
and shadow.

Grief is not just a human emotion, though there's no doubt it's one of the most damaging and unavoidable in our repertoire. We've heard of dogs who lie on their masters' graves, of elephants who touch and sniff the bones of a family member, of crows who gather for what looks like a funeral, falling silent and seeming to hold a vigil when one of their rookery has died.

Residents of Vancouver Island have been swamped with sadness seeing on the news an orca mother swimming with her dead calf, lifting it, with her nose and forehead, above the water. Her first baby and the first to be born to this pod in three years, for seventeen days she carried it and wouldn't let it go. People didn't know what to say about this tragedy acted out in our waters. "Have you seen the pictures of the whale?" they asked at the mailbox, in the grocery line-up, and then conversation stopped.

In Patrick's last book of poetry, *Washita*, there's a poem about his friend dancing with the ashes of her son cradled in her arms. Like hers, the whale's mourning was a mother's mourning and to us it felt no less. What do we lose of ourselves and what bad behaviour are we heir to and continue to impose on other species if we fail to recognize and revere their affection for their friends and kin, if we don't let into our hearts their lamentations, their suffering, their mourning? Though most days my fretting, my worry, my sadness feel only mine and human, I must remember this.

After Dickens got run over, we hired a company to surround our property with an electric wire to keep Roxy and Basho safe in our yard. Invisible Fencing, as it's called, was popular with dog owners but I talked to a woman with cats who claimed it worked equally as well. A device about the size of a Mars bar was clipped to a collar fastened around the animal's neck. When a cat or dog approached the perimeter, a small beep sounded and two seconds later, if the animal didn't move back, electrodes shot from two metal posts that touched the throat. Cruel? Yes, but if momentary pain kept the cats away from the streets, if it allowed them to be outside without the danger of being run over, Patrick and I decided it was worth it.

Roxy was a quick learner. After her training session when an instructor from the company backed her into the danger zone, let her hear the warning sound and then feel the zap, she never stepped over the boundary. Basho was a different matter. When the trainer left, he had to test it on his own, but after a couple of bad experiences, he seemed to settle into his more limited territory. One morning, however, when I looked out the window, I saw him in the neighbour's yard. I ran out, picked him up, and hustled him back home. Was his collar malfunctioning? I plunked him inside, walked to the perimeter, and swung the collar over the invisible line. The device sounded and needles of electricity pricked the palm of my hand. So what had happened? How had he crossed over? The following day I watched him crouch at the fence's perimeter almost flat to the ground, his muscles tense, then spring into the next yard. He'd learned to blast through the invisible border in the two-second pause between the beep and the shock. What a smart cat he was! What an athlete! A technician for the company came out the next day and reset the electronics so there was no delay, no time for Basho to fly through in the hesitation between the warning signal and the jolt.

The three years he lived at that house, he stayed in the yard, climbed the apple trees, slid on the snow off the deck, hid in the bushes, leapt from a standing position six feet in the air to try to snatch a bird from the feeder Patrick kept raising higher and higher. Not wanting to have to keep him inside to protect the birds, through the Audubon Society online I found a neoprene triangle to hook over his collar. He could still climb and run but it flapped when he was in motion, startled anything avian, and slowed him down enough that he couldn't snag them from their resting places. It didn't take long for him to give up on birds, and we removed the flap so that his success with rodents would continue, as it did his long life. We also got rid of the collars because we moved to a quiet dead-end street into what we thought of as the last house we'd own together.

———

How will Patrick or I survive the loss of the other? How will the one left alone get through the devastation and go on? And what of the lost one's belongings: the clothes drenched with the body's smells, the toothbrush, the eyeglasses, the watch, the leather carpenter's apron? I think of my friend who, when her husband died of esophageal cancer, though she bundled up his clothing and took it to the thrift store, couldn't bring herself to donate his shoes or get rid of the mask he wore when he went for radiation. Worried what others would think, she told no one but me.

His shoes stayed in a row on what had been his side of the closet floor. If he came home, she said, he'd need his shoes. I couldn't help but wonder where she kept the mask and what she might do with it. The thought of its physical presence, its chilling intimacy, unsettled me. Was she able to look at it? Did she take it out, lay it on his pillow? I didn't dare ask.

THE MASK

She kept the mask, not knowing
what to do with it. That hard plastic skin
moulded to the shape of his face, fitted over
his head and attached on both sides to the treatment table.
It sits in a coffee-maker box
on the closet shelf above the shoes
she's kept as well, though all the clothes
are gone. She tells no one. It's been three years—
her friends and son wouldn't understand.

Tonight she drops his shoes in a garbage bag,
relaxes her gaze, something she's learned
to do in yoga so she doesn't really see.

Then she takes down the box that promises
Maximum Capacity, Brew Strength Control,
Easy-to-Fill Water Reservoir.

She opens the lid: there it is, his face—
an empty husk, cut-outs for the mouth and nose,
none for the eyes. When asked if he wanted them,
he'd said no. She thought he'd made that choice
so he wouldn't see the blank expression
of the radiographer, the cold machine
that promised nothing. Later she wondered if,
in some strange way, he was getting ready.
Not only lying still but blind now too,
the table sliding him headfirst into a fire.

He'd practiced death so well,
when she brought him home, she kept checking
with a feather pulled from a pillow.
In the choir, he'd learned to turn a single breath
into so much sound it filled the church.
It undermined the light.

More than any photograph taken near the last,
the cast holds his likeness. She runs her fingers over
his nose, the shells of his ears, his jaw's parentheses.
What disturbs her most is the mouth, the hope-
lessness of the opening his lips surround.

She lies down on what she calls *their* bed
and dons the mask. It doesn't fit, of course,
her face is small inside it. Three years.

She trembles under the duvet that must be
stuffed with snow. Her eyes won't open.
She doesn't know how to end what she's begun.


Musicians say the music they play in front of an audience changes because of the listening in the room. Even melodies they've portrayed hundreds of times mutate and shift so that each performance is unique. When I read "The Mask" in a church hall at a literary festival in Nova Scotia, I felt the words take on a different weight and resonance. My eyes caught the gaze of a tall beautiful woman with silver-blond hair grazing her shoulders. She left the room when I finished the poem and didn't stay for the rest of the reading. She came back while I was signing books to tell me she'd lost her son two years before, and the poem had cut right through her because she'd saved his mask and because she'd done what the woman did in the poem—she'd stretched out on her bed with the mask over her face. "I'm sorry about your son," I said, "and I'm sorry the poem upset you."

"Oh, no," she said. "I had to leave for a while because I was crying, but I love the poem. It made me feel I'm not crazy." I was stunned once again by the power of poetry, by what the poem knows that the writer doesn't. My friend had kept her husband's mask but she never told me she'd worn it. I had made that part up and didn't know if it was believable. The poem had taken me there, and I had followed. And it had found a special person to speak to. It had made someone feel less alone.

November, 2018

PO CHU CURLS BESIDE ME on the couch. I rest the weight of my arm across her back, the way Patrick did when he tamed her. The bare underside of my wrist, directly in contact, picks up her purring. It must slow down my pulse, quickened daily by stress. What better soothing mechanism than a cat's deep internal vibrations, which many believe aid the animal's own healing. Some say it strengthens their bones.

Basho has stopped purring altogether. I don't know what that means. He's also stopped grooming and his long hair is matted, particularly on the side he usually lies on when he sleeps. There's no way we can tease out the thickened tangles without hurting him. The vet says all they can do is shave him. Since they can't give a cat his age an anaesthetic, he'd be uncomfortable during the removal of his hair and in any case, when it grew back in, it would probably mat again. But he might be in distress if we leave him be. Mats too close to the skin can make a cat feel the way we do if our hair is pulled by a schoolyard bully. We don't know what to do.

At five a.m. a yowl pierces my sleeping brain with the aural equivalent of a hot wire. He has never sounded so plaintive, his cry moving up and down in vowels of lament. I worry so much that it's a song of pain, and there's no way I can comfort him. When I get out of bed in the dark and kneel beside him, he falls silent but he looks confused and doesn't seem to know who I am. *Basho, Basho, Basho*, I whisper, so I won't wake Patrick—though I know that neither he nor Basho can hear. I recite under my breath Patrick's line in praise of him: "And Basho coming home, his ear torn, happy with the night." Are we hanging on to our lovely cat when we should be letting go? When will we know that it's time?

Two hours later I watch him amble like someone distracted, like someone with his head in the clouds, to his drinking spot at the pond, then weave his way through a row of deadheaded daisies. He's a pale wisp of smoke in the green vegetation, more spirit than cat, but he's outside, he's walking, he's placing his paws in familiar territory. Is it smell that guides him now, or merely the touch of his whiskers on the stones and the low shrubs that lets him know where he is? Though his sight is limited here, can he see beyond? Does he know in his blue eyes and old cat bones what's coming next? When I die, will he be there to guide me? Will I hear him purring between my final breaths? Perhaps it will be a yowl that greets me, one that brings back all the pain.

Though we live in a rainforest, the two summers and falls of Patrick's illness have been bereft of rain. When we moved from the prairies, I thought we'd never have to worry about drought again, but the trees are dying of thirst, the grass has taken on the yellow of straw, and, like in Saskatchewan, it crackles underfoot. The whole landscape is ill. Clouds of dust lift from my shoes when I walk the trails, and I crunch through the bark shed by arbutus. It resembles thin, dry paper used in stoves as tinder. Our sky is smudged with smoke, the sunsets a slow bleed because of the fires to the north, and there are what the health warnings call "particulates" in the air. As I breathe them in, I recall the dust that blocked the sun in the pages of Sinclair Ross's *As For Me and My House* and the ten years of drought in Saskatchewan that mirrored in the novel the infertility and desiccation of the marriage. It isn't our marriage that is drying out, but Patrick's well-being, his vitality. In my pagan way, I pray for the clouds to open for my beloved, who so needs to be washed by a healing rain that will also heal the earth.

One thing I know is that no matter how difficult the topic, we can't stop talking, not out of fear or the danger of hurting each other. Ours has been a relationship based on frankness, though sometimes it takes a while for us to get there. I can't help but think of the lines I wrote when he was drinking: "What changes? Lately there are things / I do not tell you—I ache inside, you / sadden me."

This last time he was admitted to the hospital he apologized for what his illness was doing to our lives. "I know I'm a ghost," he said, "even when I'm home. I'm not there for you."

"I'd rather have the ghost of you than the nothing of you," I replied.

Now he tells me he wonders if he is dying. Twenty years ago our friend who'd been diagnosed with stomach cancer asked, "Is this what dying feels like?" It turned out it was, but how were we to know? I've asked myself the same question but never voiced it out loud. I hold one of his bruised hands with both of my own, and say, "I've wondered that too." And we both cry.

Patrick is talking more and more about this garden being his last. When interviewed in our gazebo for the book *Beauty by Design* he said, "After this, I'll be a demented old man living in a small room. Lorna, I hope, will still be with me. But even then I'd have a garden. As long as there's a window with light coming through, I'd have a little bonsai tree. A small hollowed-out rock, a bit of volcanic pumice stone, a tree, and a bit of moss. That's a full garden. You can make a garden in a thimble."

How could I not adore a man who talks like this? I want to be with the person he is now and the person he'll become, no matter who that may be. I must find a way to tell him this so that he'll believe it and stop worrying so much about me as our time together unwinds towards its end. Dennis Lee's brief plea could be imprinted on my skin:

> Tell the ones you love, you
> love them;
> tell them now.
> For the day is coming, and also the night will come,
> when you will neither say it, nor hear it, nor care.

Twenty-one years ago, when I showed up at my first Al-Anon meeting, I knew that walking through that church door was an admittance that Patrick was an alcoholic and that I was going crazy because I didn't know what to do. He was still drinking heavily and didn't attend meetings himself. That made me angry. I wanted to shout, "Why am I the one seeking help? It's you who needs it, not me." Little did I know. Al-Anon taught me how to live a better life, how to admit I could save no one but me, how to cobble together my own serenity and happiness whether Patrick continued drinking or not.

The door I walk through now is the front entrance of a different church and Patrick's been sober for almost two decades, but I need help just the same. It's not Al-Anon, but a gathering for caregivers, specifically for those who live with a spouse with Parkinson's.

I didn't know that before I arrived. There are five women, including me, and two men. The wife of one of them was diagnosed only six months ago. He says they still feel optimistic and, in fact, are going to Hawaii in a month. A tall, lanky woman I'll call Monica—I guess she's in her early eighties—has been living with her husband's diagnosis for twenty-seven years. Much of the conversation is about the disease itself and various drugs and treatments their spouses have tried. I notice that when the caregivers refer to things like this, they use the pronoun "we," not "he" or "she." It is "we" who are trying a new way of lessening the amount of protein consumed in a day, "we" who are doing better with a tube in the stomach that delivers the necessary dose more quickly, "we" who are going to a doctor in Vancouver.

This conflation of the caregiver's self with his or her ill partner scares me. Is this what happens? Does all independence, do all signs of an autonomous life disappear? I'm also uneasy with one husband's belief that he knows what's best for his wife. She's balking at an operation that will insert a tube in her stomach and into her bowel (did I hear that right?) and thus make the absorption of the drug Sinemet more efficient. He wants her to have the procedure done though there are risks, one of them infection around the site. When I ask if he worries he's interfering, if he wonders if he should back down and let her make the decision because she's the one who's sick, two other people in the room answer for him. It's his role to lead her to the choice he favours, they say, in different words though the meaning's clear—the ill person is often incapable of doing what is right for her.

I've been so careful not to pressure Patrick. Though I want him to get another opinion, see a naturopath, consult a physiotherapist, et cetera, I have backed off from pushing him where he doesn't want to go. Am I being too delicate, too respectful? How can I be sure that in the middle of his cognitive confusion and his physical challenges he knows what's best for him? What should a good wife or husband do? Is my respect for his independence a kind of neglect? Or is it cowardice because I'm afraid my advice might be wrong and then I'll be blamed?

When it's Monica's turn to share her story, the woman around my age who's running the group asks if she's still painting. "No," Monica says, and I feel a stab in my gut. The facilitator turns to me, the newcomer, and says, "Monica does beautiful paintings. She used to show in a gallery in Vancouver." After the meeting has ended, I deliberately match the taller woman's stride as we walk out of the church. I ask if she minds talking to me for a moment before we get in our cars. "May I ask why you've stopped painting?" I say.

"I'm tired out," she replies, as if there's nothing more to add. Her face looks as worn as old linen rubbed thin between two fingers day after day, as wrinkled as drawing paper left out in the rain then set in the sun to dry.

Maybe I should drop it, but I feel compelled to ask if it's okay with her, to give up her art. "It hurts me not to paint. Almost as much," she goes on, "as seeing my husband the way he is." She bobs her chin in the direction of a stooped man who, with great effort, drags his almost unworkable legs toward a parked SUV. Those with Parkinson's had a meeting at the same time in the same building, just in a different room. It's hard to watch him through any eyes—but especially through hers. "He used to be such an athlete."

Of course, I've made her loss personal. I'm worrying what will happen to my writing if I'm worn to nothing by Patrick's illness. I can't help but think of Tennessee Williams's treatise on love, which I'd come across on the website *Brain Pickings*: "The world is violent and mercurial—it will have its way with you. We are saved only

by love—love for each other and the love that we pour into the
art we feel compelled to share: being a parent; being a writer;
being a painter; being a friend. We live in a perpetually burning
building, and what we must save from it, all the time, is love."
From that perpetually burning building, is there time and energy
to rescue both the person and the art? Or does one of them have
to go up in flames?

## INSIDE A NEEDLE

This summer, night comes to her
as a large animal, breathing. Warm and damp
where its breath meets her skin.

Too much time near a sick bed
creates another sickness, sweats and chills
and a high fever for the past.

The deadless man lives inside a needle inside an egg
inside a duck inside a rabbit. That sounds right
though the folklore is not her own.

Don't say your life is ending.
There's a woman at your door
with three round loaves of bread.

The mind's gone soft from spending hours
on feather pillows. Who is forgetting you
so perfectly today?

———

Our back-yard pond is populated by goldfish and two turtles. They're red-eared sliders, *Trachemys scripta elegans*. It's a fanciful name for what, until recently, was the most common reptile sold in pet stores in the U.S. and Canada. I wonder if *scripta* comes from the unique hieroglyphs scrawled across the bottom of their shells. If *elegans* comes from the graceful way each turtle stretches out one back leg when it basks in the sun like a dancer at the barre.

For at least three decades, this slow-moving reptile served as an easy-to-care-for alternative to kittens and puppies. When they outgrew their aquariums, many a family, bored by their inactivity and seeming indifference to humans, dropped them off at the closest creek or slough. In the case of what we've come to call *our* turtles, the previous owners of the house came up with a kinder alternative that had a better chance of ensuring their survival—they set them free into their newly excavated pond. When we moved into the house in December, but for the midwinter, sluggish flicker of fish, the water looked uninhabited—but a note on the kitchen counter let us know the turtles, though invisible, were there. They'd sunk into the shallow muck at the bottom in mid-October and would stay inactive for six to seven months, not hibernating, we learned when we did some research, but *brumating*.

That was a new word for me, and I've grown to love it. It makes me think of ruminating, a reptilian, philosophical sinking into a six-month Zen of cold and mud. Do they brumate / ruminate on whether they are turtles dreaming winter, or winter dreaming turtles? Catching sight of them for the first time March or April hallelujahs spring's arrival. For us it's more exhilarating than the first yellow of the daffodils or the white and purple of crocus buds blurting from the soil. One of us will spot them and cry out, "The turtles! The turtles are back!" As if they've returned from a long arduous journey. Perhaps they have.

The turtles, we were told, are both female—the only sex sold across B.C. The absence of males means zero reproduction for these imports from the Mississippi River and the Gulf of Mexico; otherwise the offspring could overwhelm the population of indigenous testudines found in every corner of the province. Since the previous owners of the house didn't leave us with the turtles' names, we decided to christen them after women writers we admired: the larger of the two, the size of a generous dinner plate, became Drabble.

A few years after her christening, I sat across the table from Sir Michael Holroyd, the husband of Margaret Drabble, at a dinner at the International Festival of Authors in Toronto. I excitedly broke through his British reserve to tell him we'd named one of our turtles after his wife because we loved her writing. "I shall tell Margaret," he said. "I believe she will be pleased." The name "Drabble" suits a turtle. Its double b's mimic the reptile's *bonk, bonk,* across the stones and its plop into the water. I could only hope my favourite British novelist would be pleased.

I didn't tell Sir Michael that we named the second turtle Byatt, after A.S. Byatt, Drabble's feuding sister and the author of *Possession*. Perhaps using the names of two siblings who didn't like each other and had expressed their animosity publicly brought the reptiles bad luck, because during our second summer in the house, Byatt disappeared. A neighbour found her lumbering down his driveway to the road and kindly returned her to the pond. A week later, she escaped a second time, in all likelihood forcing herself through a slight dip at the bottom of the fence and heading off to greener waters. We never saw her again.

For both turtles, the attempt to run away from home is a yearly event. In mid-summer some switch turns to "On" inside their cold-blooded bodies and the desire to ensure the continuation of their species mercilessly harries them to find a spot to lay their eggs. For reasons we don't understand, the shore around the pond and its long apron are not suitable, though Patrick hauled in sand to build a nesting ground away from the water that looked hospitable, at least to us, for a reptile nursery. After Byatt's vanishing act, not wanting to lose Drabble or allow her to invade the habitation of native species like the Painted and the Northern Pacific Pond, Patrick had nailed boards along the bottom of the fence surrounding the pond and barricaded the walkways that connected this bit of the yard with the larger section to the side and at the back.

Drabble is now contained, but every July she pulls herself out of the water, trundles to the palings and bangs into them, searching for a gap. She's driven by an imperative to reach her imagined nesting site though there's been no male to mate with her, to tuck his semen in her shell to anoint the eggs as they pass through. It's heartbreaking to watch her yearly attempt to break free so she can reproduce. One of us will find her yards from the pond, lift her by the edges of her shell, and carry her back, holding her as far away from our torsos as our arms can stretch because she always lets loose a stream of pee, the underside of her carapace decorated with what she's dragged herself over—pine needles, dirt, dry bamboo leaves, the petals of low-lying flowers. Within half an hour she'll be at it again. I did a double take when I came upon her on a summer afternoon on the hardwood floor in the middle of our front hall. The back door had been left open and she'd waddled inside. I don't know if the eggs wither inside her or if she finally drops them into pockets of the earth somewhere in the yard. We've never found them. Within a few weeks, she settles down and her desperate need to escape her beautiful prison suddenly stops.

Not liking to see a creature on its own, after Byatt moved on Patrick found two saucer-sized female turtles at a pet store. They were the last, the owner told him, he'd be able to bring in. We called them Emily (after Emily Dickinson) and Brontë. They grew quickly to the circumference of bread plates and seemed to thrive. One morning we found Brontë lying about five feet away from the pond on a mound of moss. Three of her legs were pulled into her shell. The fourth dangled, ragged and torn. At the animal clinic, the vet informed us that the three legs we couldn't see weren't tucked away, but had been chewed off, probably by a mink. He suggested, and we agreed, that he'd put her down.

It's difficult to think of a turtle being skittish, but after the horrible attack on Brontë, Emily would drop off the stones into the water if even a shadow came near. Drabble, older and larger, seemed unaffected. Patrick had seen the mink a few weeks before, as graceful in its swimming as a dark, muscled rope lashing through the water. He clapped his hands and shouted. It gave him a fierce look and slipped with little haste away.

The mink reminded us that the pond, for all the tranquility and pleasure it gives us, is a murderous site. The first time we saw a great blue heron standing still near the shore as if a painter had stroked its image on the water with a delicate brush, we thought a Japanese scroll had come to life. We were delighted. Then we spotted a large koi in its beak and, before we could run out the door and scare the tall bird off, it bashed the fish against the rocks.

Another morning, the water lily pots were tipped, the marsh marigolds ripped apart, the fish so spooked we thought the pond was empty. Had a heron gone berserk? On the edge was what I mistook for an orange Creamsicle. It was the head of one of our oldest koi, which we'd transported from our former house, the fish we'd called the Golden One. Two days before, I'd seen an otter lounging in the sun on the deck outside our bedroom door. She looked like a plump courtesan waiting for a servant to bring figs, chocolates, and perfumed Turkish towels. We sat quietly on the other side of the glass and marvelled at her sleek, plush splendour. She found, however, a way around to the back. She found the pond. Now we were faced with a new dilemma.

Patrick banged together a gate at the end of the driveway that ran along the side of the house. There hadn't been a gate there before because it was where we'd back the truck and, with the wheelbarrow, haul debris to dump into the box and take for recycling. His carpentry finished in a few hours, Patrick was sure the otter wouldn't be able to get to the pond from that direction. The next morning, the waters were ransacked again. There was a dip at the bottom of the gate—the otter had burrowed under. We called a wildlife officer to ask about a live trap. He said the only place to put one would be at the bottom of the pond—"live" trap in this case would be a misnomer—the otter would drown. "What if we leave it?" we asked. "Will it abandon the pond after it eats the fish?"

"If there's nothing else, it will go for the turtles. It will snap them in half and devour the meat."

For a moment, Patrick wished he hadn't given away his father's rifle. How easily we turned into murderers, we thought. We didn't want to lose our fish, our turtles—but were they more valuable than the wild animal whom a few days ago we'd found so beautiful?

After a few hours of soul searching, we decided against the trap. Patrick dug below the gate and I helped him pour cement into the trench. We then walked around the fence that surrounded the yard, looking for any gaps an otter could slither through. Patrick pounded in boards, we dragged Cindercrete blocks and pushed them in front of any openings. For now the turtles and fish were safe. The invasion was a reminder of the vulnerability of the pond and garden, so close to the ocean and the forest. We had tricked ourselves into thinking we were in control, into believing we could protect what we cared for. We hadn't factored in herons and otters and weasels. We hadn't entertained the possibility of an illness breaking down the gates and fences we'd tried to build around each other.

Something strange happens to time when you live with illness. Days are defined by doctors' appointments, often three in one week on top of heart or bone or lung scans and blood tests booked at the hospital. Our hours have been kidnapped by medical demands. But it's more than that—neither of us has any sense of duration, of how many weeks or months have passed. When did certain symptoms start and how long have they been going on? When was Patrick's last stay in the hospital—October or November? How many times has he been admitted this past year and a half? How many weeks have gone by since he could walk to the end of the driveway, how many months since food tasted good? When did we last book a dinner reservation, see a movie in a theatre, when did we make love? Prisoners of his illness, we've rarely ventured out, accepting things like dinner invitations from friends only with their understanding that we might cancel at the last minute. There's no way to predict the day before or even the morning of the event whether Patrick will have the strength to go out.

The divisions of the day take on a different meaning than they used to: early morning, before he wakes up, I bask in a slender beam of hope as the first of the sun slips through the window of the kitchen where I sip a cup of coffee, the house silent. It's a glass bell of sanctuary and quiet. I don't know yet if he's feeling better than yesterday or worse. I haven't had the chance to ask. Night comes as a release: it means on simple terms that we've made it through the hours without forgetting his medication, without an emergency, without a collapse, and we can go to bed, Patrick with a sleeping pill so I don't have to worry about his being restless, me with an e-reader I hold off my side of the mattress and close to the floor so the light won't bother him.

He seems to have given up on time completely. I'm the one who watches the clock, ensuring we leave the house with enough leeway, depending on the traffic, to make it downtown for the next appointment. Usually, I get us there early. Sitting in a waiting room feels like drifting on a raft down a sluggish, too-warm river, neither of us talking, not even bothering to lift a magazine from the wide coffee table. I can't bear to read about the triumphs and vacuous tragedies of movie stars and members of the royal family. Patrick slouches in an expensive chair if we're in a specialist's office, or in a cheap vinyl substitute if we're in a lab or outpatients' clinic, his eyes closed, waiting for his name to be called. I don't know what he is thinking.

Since I'm our official timekeeper, it's lucky I've always liked wearing a watch, and a big one at that. When my father died, the only things of his I asked for were an old, rusty El Camino and his watch. Not the gold-banded Seiko he wore at the end of his life, urging my mother to set it to the correct time even when he didn't know the day or month. I wanted the watch he'd dropped in the kitchen drawer that housed things of little or no use: a broken nutcracker, elastic bands, a paring knife with a busted handle, the collar and tags of the dog who'd died. Dad wore the watch when he was younger and worked at hard labour, driving backhoes and Cats—first for the city of Swift Current, then for small, privately owned companies in the oil patch. The watch had a blue face and a thick leather band, darker on the inside because of his sweat, the oils from his skin, and the dirt from the fields. It had known so intimately his inner wrist, its excrescences, its temperatures, its pulse. But what I liked best was its mechanism. One of the earliest automatics, it depended on the wearer's movement to keep it going. If you took it off, as he had done, it would slow down and eventually stop.

With new holes punched in the strap so it would fit me—although it looked huge above my hand, much smaller than my father's—the watch felt heavy and significant, as if his ghost encircled the bones of my wrist with his once-strong fingers. I wore it every day until it broke down, the jeweller unable to find replacement parts. For at least three years my body had kept it going after my father's had fallen still. There was something satisfying in my being the source of its power, its almost silent *tick, tick, tick*.

I can't help but think of the seconds, minutes, hours my father's watch would have lost were it strapped to Patrick's wrist. Curled up in bed most of the day and night, his body doesn't have the power to keep itself going, let alone animate the workings of a watch, its blue flat face blankly counting out our new blurred relationship with time.


I have been with Patrick for more than half my life. We lived together for twenty-three years before we got married in the back garden of our former house in Saanichton, the setting for Patrick's memoir and our home for fifteen years. It was an odd wedding, under the apple tree. We both felt shy, not knowing if it was the right thing to do, and we invited only ten friends, no one from either family although Patrick's two sons lived in town and my mother was a short flight away. I don't know if Patrick's sons or my mother were hurt, but I know she was relieved that we'd made things official. She hated it whenever, interviewed on national radio, we denied being married. It embarrassed her; she wanted us to lie. She also worried about my legal status. Would I have the same rights as a wife if Patrick died, she asked, or would his two exes and five adult children swoop in and scoop up everything?

In our favourite restaurant Patrick, out of the blue, had slid across the table a small card. Inside he'd written, "Will you marry me?" With the card was a package he told me to open. A narrow box held a necklace of flat turquoise stones and a small frog carved out of a single chunk of the same stone. I was taken aback. "I'll have to think about it," I said. His look of dismay and hurt made me quickly say, "Okay, if you want to." An unenthusiastic reply, not because I doubted the rightness of our relationship, but because I worried about changing it. Would our being together become something we'd take for granted? For over two decades, unmarried, we'd stayed with each other because we wanted to, not because of some official or religious sanction. We'd chosen companionship, we'd chosen to be together day by day by day.

Patrick said he proposed because he'd been six months without a drink and, as a sober man, he wanted to make a new commitment to me. AA recommends you shouldn't make any major decisions in your first year of recovery. Patrick ignored that advice.

Our vows beneath the apple tree, Roxy and Basho stretched out in the dappled sun beneath its branches, were poems. Patrick opened his, "Little Bones," with these lines:

Twenty-three years and still the hours go
from dawn to dusk as if they know
something I don't. I never wanted time, that tyranny,
the years I lacked restraint, thought excess
love, refused the past by holding it too close,
dreamed yesterday was damage done.
I drank it daily. Some say the broken

never heal, and sometimes when I rise
I feel that scars are my body's measure.

I heard the resolve in his words: his desire to stand with me
without the pale curse of vodka coursing through his veins and gut,
without the lies such an obsession brings. One hand trembled as
he held the paper and read; the other gripped mine so tightly I
thought he'd crush my fingers. I replied:

These are the days of dahlias
and sunflowers, of nuthatches hiding seeds in lichen
on the bark, the days when we begin to notice
the lessening of the light. Light's an abundance
I was born to. So much of it, I learned
to walk the open, eyes half shut. Even then
or completely blind, I'd know you by your smell,
I'd know you by your hands on me, the scars
I'd touch on your wide forehead.
. . .

We never published the poems: if we'd asked the other to edit
them, they wouldn't have passed muster. But they said for us in
that moment in the garden, in front of our two cats and our friends,
all we were capable of saying and needed to say. Nothing changed
after the wedding: we lived in the same house, we did the same
things, but a sweetness that wasn't there before slipped inside us.
We teased each other about how cozy we'd become, and how
amused we were to use the names "my husband," "my wife."

———

Before this sad, doomed twin called Patrick-Terribly-Ill arrived, we were stricken with the probability that he was going blind. The diagnosis had been irrefutable: macular degeneration, the dry kind as opposed to the wet—for the dry there is no treatment. On the ophthalmologist's orders, Patrick pinned a graph on the wall above his printer. To me the vertical and horizontal lines could have been drawn by an expert draughtsman with a straight-edged ruler. They never shifted and there was nothing more precise and sure. In his eyes, sometimes the lines wavered. If they wobbled so much that it seemed as if they'd succumbed to vertigo, he was to make another appointment with the doctor. Otherwise Patrick wouldn't see him for a year because there was nothing that could be done.

Over several months Patrick wrote about the fear of blindness; I did too. Ironically, as a child, before anyone figured out he needed glasses, he thought his blurry vision was normal. The stars he saw were Van Gogh's energetic spirals exploding into outer space. Snow rising in the wind from the drifts on the frozen lake were the wings of winter swans. When he was fitted with the proper lenses toward the end of grade one, his corrected eyesight was, in some ways, a disappointment.

We worried that Patrick might lose his driver's license and talked about the need to move out of our rural neighbourhood and closer to a bus route. He promised me he wouldn't fake it—when he knew his vision was too poor for him to drive, he'd tell me.

Now that so many other symptoms are beating up his body, macular degeneration, and its possible debilitating end, never come up. It's as if the affliction has gone away. Sure, he's had to abandon reading books and he no longer drives, though he used to be the one that drove us everywhere. But it's not the diminishment of his sight that has brought about these changes. It's his physical weakness and his inability to process what's going on in the flow of traffic or the narrative of a book. Yet isn't it odd, I say to myself, that his inevitable blindness—something once so terrifying—concerns neither of us anymore? It goes to show how serious all this other stuff is, how, in comparison, his becoming blind is not the worst thing we will have to face.

## SELF-CENTRED

My husband is going blind.

Soon no one will say
I am beautiful

in my new dress,
my red shoes.

Or will he say it more often,
old woman that I am,

now that he can't see?

The middle of November, six a.m., the moon's blue-white glow buffing the frost on the neighbour's roof. Ours must have been frosted too, but from inside the kitchen I couldn't see it. I was waiting until seven to call the vet. Patrick was in the hospital again, the fourth time since March. I didn't know how much more he could take. When he sees me close to tears, he quotes Julian of Norwich: "All shall be well, and all shall be well, and all manner of things shall be well." I fall into the rhythm of the refrain, so oft repeated. Does he say this just to comfort me, or does he have faith he'll get better, that we'll continue to have the blessings of each other? I want to believe it; I want him to believe it too. On the other hand, he could be reciting this to teach me a kind of zen-like acceptance. Whatever will come, will come. There's nothing I can do, all shall be well.

A week ago, I'd dropped off Basho at our usual animal clinic for the vet technician to look at the mats in his coat and, if she could do it without hurting him, get rid of any that were causing him pain. He came home with his sides and back shorn. She said there were bruises on his skin where the knotted hair had been pulling when he moved. Even with partial baldness, he looked so handsome. With a thick muff around his chin and the top of his neck, he could have been a miniature lion camouflaged for snow, not the yellow grass of the plains. When I ran my hands over his exposed skin, it felt like rich velvet had replaced his long, fine hair. For a few days he seemed more mobile, and he began eating with little coaxing from me, but I worried he'd get a chill because he had no protection on his skinny flanks. Though it was cold outside, he went out anyway to patrol his territory. It pleased me so to watch him walk up the path and bend down, with his shoulders hunched, over the pond to drink.

On this mid-November morning I was waiting to call Marilyn, the vet I'd met several years ago at a sunrise yoga class that didn't exist anymore. She specializes in house calls and palliative care. I'd been building a relationship with her—twice a week, whenever Patrick was in the hospital, she'd show up to give Basho his intravenous water. I wanted her to get to know him so when the time came, I wouldn't have to take him to a clinic, and he could die at home with a vet who was his friend.

The last time Marilyn had pulled out the needle and folded up the tubing, Basho turned his head away from the treats he usually begged for. The day after, I couldn't find him. I searched under the beds, behind the desks and couches, in the darkest corners. I walked the garden calling his name though I knew he couldn't hear. Finally, late afternoon, he showed up, went directly to his litter box and lay there. He'd never done this before. I phoned Marilyn and she came by again to give him a shot of antibiotics: cats with kidney failure often succumb to bladder infections, she said. She also gave him something for pain and left me with medicine to squirt into his mouth if I sensed he was hurting, even in the middle of the night.

For the first time since we'd moved to this house, Basho didn't sit on my lap in the library early evening but flopped on his fleecy pad on top of the loveseat across the room, where warmth rose from the electric heater. I turned up the thermostat before I went to bed. Usually he'd join me in about an hour or so, and when Patrick was there beside me, he'd sink between us, immobile as a soft stone until around midnight when he'd rise, stand near my pillow and stare. Without opening my eyes, I'd reach to my nightstand for his bowl of crunchies and place it near his head. When he finished feeding, half asleep, I'd put it back and cover it with the thin hardcover book of poems by Stephen Dunn that served as a lid so Po couldn't raid his stash. Some people called me crazy for waking up two, three times a night to feed Basho but before Po, when we could leave his bowl of food on the floor, he was used to frequent snacks whenever he felt hungry. To hear him crunch the hard pellets was one of the most comforting sounds in the world.

A night ago, he'd slept with me but didn't wake me and at breakfast he'd only licked the soft food I put in his dish. Tonight, though I called him, he didn't show up at all. Nor did I hear him yowl. I knew something had shifted in the house because when

I woke around 1 a.m., it was Po Chu who curled beside me, her warmth pressing into the curve of my belly. The bed had been Basho's territory. Normally, even if he wasn't stretched out on our mattress, she wouldn't dare venture here, let alone settle down and purr. Afraid to get up and check on him and find he'd died while I was sleeping, I made myself lie in the dark, Po beside me, until four a.m.

Basho was where I saw him last, on the top of the back of the couch. He was breathing, but he didn't move when I ran my hand over his cheek and down his suede-like shorn back. His eyes were dull, and he didn't make a sound. The absence of the yowls I once found disturbing was worse than the sound itself. I waited until just before dawn, around seven a.m, then called Marilyn. She said she'd be over within the hour. It was the moment I'd been dreading, and I'd have to do it without Patrick by my side.

I had texted him before I'd gone to bed to let him know Basho was near the end. "I'm so sorry, Babe, I'm not with you," he replied. He'd had a bad day, tests delayed because someone forgot to stop the blood thinners, a new doctor he'd never seen asking the same questions, not reading his file. Another doctor's name he couldn't remember. And he wasn't rallying like before, just getting thinner and more despondent. I tried my best to sound strong for him, to muster the strength to face what lay ahead at home.

Basho lies on a blanket on the library floor, Marilyn and I kneeling on either side of him. It takes about fifteen minutes for him to drop into sleep from the anaesthetic.

I slide my cheek over his shaved back and along his ribs. I nuzzle. Eighteen years, eighteen years with this beautiful boy, this graceful, feral companion. He should have been a movie star, I say to Marilyn. He was a star in *your* life, she says. I keep glancing at his face to see if he's closed his eyes. He probably won't, she says.

Po Chu walks by, making the funny squeak that is her version of a meow. She sniffs Marilyn's bag and rubs her cheeks against it, walks around Basho's inert form but doesn't go directly to him. Basho's eyes remain half open.

If you're ready, she says, I'll give him the injection.

A few minutes after, she uses her stethoscope to check his heart. It's still beating. It will be soon, she says.

You've seen this so often. What happens to an animal's spirit when it dies?

I don't know, she says.

I tell her about the writer Jim Harrison's idea of heaven: a white two-storey house in the country. He's walking down a road toward it and it's full of all the animals he's ever loved. For me that would be the two dogs I had as a kid, Tiny and Spike; the beagle from my first marriage, Gimli; and then, with Patrick, our four cats: Nowlan, Dickens, Roxy, and Basho. As I walk down the road toward them, will they hear me coming? Will their nostrils twitch with my familiar smell? Will they rise and wait at the door for it to open, their ears alert to my footfalls on the step?

I hope I'll see him again, I say to her. Maybe Roxy has come to meet him. After all, he lived with her for his first fourteen years.

People, she says, talk about guardians, loved ones who arrive to help them on their way. Why can't animals have them too?

She checks his heart again. It's stopped beating. I've heard that a cat, in the room with someone dying, will sense when the soul is about to leave the body. The animal will leap on the bed and some-times lie on the human's chest. I wonder what creature—invisible to my eye—might arrive for Basho. A dragonfly? A moth dusting his small chest? The smallest of tree frogs. A black and white spotted cat?

Marilyn leaves me with a candle, instructions for burial, and phone numbers of grief counsellors I can call if I need them. I light the candle and sit with Basho. I tell him what a wonderful cat he was. I rest my head lightly on his long skinny body, feeling his softness against my face. My dear one, my noble cat.

I have never thought of him as a child or a substitute for one, but I have loved him deeply and I am broken by this loss. The bond is multi-layered and profound—unlike my link with other humans, our connection crosses species. Little in my DNA matches his, but we have been companions through the seasons, in two different gardens and houses, on the paths of Patrick's drunkenness and sobriety, his sickness and his health. Basho's been with us in our happiness and our despair. Alongside each other we have slept through the hours, he on my lap or beside me in the bed, our dreams weaving together their warp and weft above our heads. His sharp senses have ignited mine, alerting my narrow sight to what catches his eye, making me take notice. He has expanded my world, pushing the edges of my narrow perception to include his sense of being and knowing, his at-homeness in the yard he's marked as his own. I've been made larger by his presence, just as I've been made larger by Patrick's.

Patrick's son Michael comes to help me dig the grave. Though I'm strong from lifting weights at the gym three days a week, I didn't think I could hack through the cement-like clay that supports the thin layer of topsoil. I had to find a dry spot so water wouldn't course through and carry any contaminants from the lethal injection that sits in his body. The grave is also supposed to be four feet down so no animal, including eagles, will ingest the poison. Michael has an aging cat, so he knows what I am feeling. We hug and cry. He's built like Patrick, the same leanness, the same wide shoulders. When he wraps his arms around me and the side of my face presses into his chest, he feels like his father. Though shorter than Patrick, he too rests his chin on my head.

You're the closest thing I have to your dad today, I tell him. I'm so glad you're here.

While he digs the grave I search our shelves for a book by David Elliott, the late Newfoundland poet. The poem I'm looking for is an elegy for a cat named Frank and I've never forgotten the ending: "He could, all by himself, open the door to the garden."

Though there's little time, I want to write my own tribute to Basho. Surely a cat who has lived with two poets for eighteen years deserves his own poem. I quickly pull something together, then go back outside. Michael lowers Basho on his sleeping pad into the cavity in the earth. I ask him to read David's "Frank," then, my voice breaking, I begin to recite. I will get through this, I will do it for him and for Patrick, who can't be here with us.

THE CAT WE CALLED BASHO
  *(d. Nov. 17, 2018, 8:05 a.m.)*

Though he deigned to live with us for eighteen years
I didn't know until the vet arrived with the injection
he's called a lynx-point, because of his colouring and the tabby
markings on his face, she said. I would add because of the hair
that sprouts from his brown-tipped ears and because his coat
is thick enough for the coldest winters—it looks as if it's rimed
    with frost,
so bright it is when the sun combs through. Surely
he's a lynx-point too because of his nature. Though he was kind to us
he never lost his wildness. Rabbits bled out on our hall rug
after he chewed off their heads; all that remained of the rats
he caught in the garden and lugged through the high window

were the bile ducts and the tails. Then there were his big paws and the long tufts between his toes—so he could walk on snow and not fall through.

There's no way to prepare yourself for the sound and sight of earth falling on a body. It is your naked heart lying there, the dirt landing hard and cold.

Patrick is home after almost a month in the hospital. There's no Basho to greet him, no Basho in his office. There's been a diminishment in our house, a terrible lessening in our surroundings and in my beloved's body. Wasted by this mysterious disease, shrunken, Patrick's not strong enough to go outside with me, even with his walker, to stand beside the newly dug grave, to light the candle I partly burned the day Basho died, and sprinkle a pinch of tobacco a friend has left us. If you live long enough, love long enough, you lose parents and friends, you lose cats, one of you will inevitably lose the other. Patrick says to me, "I think it was a good thing you had to deal with Basho on your own."

"Why?" I ask.

"I don't know." But he does know and I do too. He means I'm going to have to deal soon with more than the death of our cat. He wants me to be strong for what lies ahead. This is the closest we've come to talking about this bone-chilling inevitability and it scares me so.

I don't know how much time he and I have left together. What I do know is how lucky we are to have had four decades. At the best, can we expect two or three years? Should I be thinking of months? Daily I read the obituaries in our local paper, track the deaths of strangers and those I know, figure out their ages and compare them to Patrick's. This is my new macabre math. A math made out of fear. If people younger than him can pass away, then he can too. I delight when I hear of longevity—writers and artists who live and work into their eighties. Al Purdy, who was our friend; Ursula Le Guin, whom I once met, and who chose my selected poems as her summer reading, Margaret Drabble and Mary Pratt; and far away in time and place, Henri Matisse, cutting shapes with scissors when he could no longer control a brush. In her house in Holland Park in London, P.D. James's keen mind kept her poet-detective, Adam Dalgliesh, detecting into her ninth decade. There's some hope in that.

When Carol Shields died in 2003, a year after her novel *Unless* was published, she was a decade younger than Patrick is now. I hadn't seen her for a few weeks and heard about her death while I was at a writers' retreat at a Benedictine monastery about seventy-five minutes north and east of Saskatoon. It's a working farm with cattle and chickens, a big vegetable garden, an orchard, and fields of wheat, hay, and canola. One of the monks approached our group of eight writers at the breakfast table and told us that he had heard the news of a famous writer's death on CBC radio earlier that morning. He wondered if any of us had known her.

Even though you know something is inevitable, when it happens, it still comes as a surprise. Part of you feels stunned and looks around for meaning and significance, for some kind of sign to match your sadness and mark the change that's taken place. The night Carol died, a fierce wind had blown through the monastery grounds, had awakened me and kept me tossing in bed until sunrise. In the morning, in the huge old cottonwood outside my window, the wind continued to roil and thrash as if the tree wouldn't let it go, its big-leafed branches whipping with the effort. I couldn't help but see the frenzied motion as a powerful spirit trying to leave the world. Though it was early, before eight a.m., I poured myself a glass of wine and stood under the green roar. I toasted Carol, then threw the rest of the wine against the runnelled trunk, wishing her an unimpeded journey when she broke free from all that wanted to hold her and, heading east, rolled across the prairies all the way to Winnipeg, then south to Chicago and home.

Later the same day, one of the other writers who'd been at the breakfast table when we'd heard of Carol's death, a young poet about to publish her first book, was walking the dirt road that ran between a group of barns and sheds. She had never met Carol but she'd read her books and, over the years, had listened to her on CBC. Daydreaming her way into a poem, gazing at the clouds that scudded past, she suddenly heard Carol's voice. Eerily distinct and clear, it wafted through the air above the sound of the wind. It seemed to be coming from the long, narrow shed a few yards ahead of her and to the left.

Hesitant and slightly scared, she walked towards it. The door of the shed was missing though a grid of wire was nailed across the opening so nothing could go in or out. Carol's voice was louder now. She was reading from *Larry's Party*. The young woman recognized the passage about Larry leading his small son through the maze he had built in his back yard. She peered through the door into the darkness, not knowing what she'd see.

From inside the shed, came the clucking of hens. Dozens of them walked the floor near the back, placing their feet with precision as if they knew ahead of time where each foot should fall, as if they woke up every morning with maps glued to the bottom of their toes. Dozens more roosted in the rafters, and at the very back of the shed, on a white plastic pail turned upside down, sat a big transistor radio. Although the woman couldn't see the dial she knew it had to be set on CBC, Carol reading, "It may be that Larry has romanticized this particular memory. The soft kiss of the evening sun, the dizzy, unalarming purr of mosquitoes in his ear, his little boy's hand in his. . . ."

The smell of the coop drifted through the wire as she stood and listened: a whiff of wet feathers though they were dry, dust shuffled by the chickens' feet, an acrid pungency from the soft white droppings that streaked the rafters and spotted the floor. With the smell, Carol's mellifluous voice floated in the air above the glottal sound of hens. It is common knowledge that many farmers play tapes of Beethoven and Mozart in dairy barns to settle the cows and make them give more milk. The CBC voices and music that came from the radio must have been there to relax the hens and encourage them to lay.

During that day of tributes and Carol's elegantly tuned, considered sentences winding to the end of thought, in the long dark shed in the monastery yard, the hens were laying eggs. Inside each shell would be the warm glow of her voice, the flavour of her speaking. I wish I could tell Carol this story. She would have loved knowing that her writing and reading had been put to good use, that her voice had gone to such a place. For the next few mornings at breakfast, I paused for a moment after I'd lopped off the top of my soft-boiled eggs as if there were a sound caught inside and about to be released. If I listened hard enough, perhaps I'd hear a word as tasty and numinous as *unless*.

## February, 2019

ALMOST TWO YEARS since Patrick's first collapse, the 911 call, the rush to emergency. This February, four feet of snow have fallen in our yard. It's buried the daffodil buds, the snowdrop blossoms, the clenched fists of tulips. The rest of the country is laughing at us on the west coast. We don't know what to do with snow. The schools shut down, the power goes out as a tree falls on the line, cars slide off the roads in a kind of mad winter choreography.

I start to dig out our long driveway but I'm met halfway by our eighty-year-old neighbour who finishes the task with his snow blower. Three times I've gone out for two-hour shifts in my lime-green gumboots to bang the drifts off the shrubs and trees with a broom so the branches won't break. Snow nudges down my collar and up my sleeves as it did when I was a child in Saskatchewan. I take some joy in that.

There's so much snow it's easy to imagine us and our raincoast habitat spun round and round in a soft cocoon. I can't help but hope we'll transmogrify before the weather breaks, emerge as a revived healthy pair of creatures flexing our new wings. It's lucky Roxy isn't here to catch us in flight and bring us down from the sky.

If we ever had wings, they're now torn and frayed. Patrick's day shift is as monotonous as a low-end factory worker's: get up early, have breakfast, go back to bed, have a bath, go back to bed, work on email, go back to bed, and on and on and on. At the kitchen table we eat the supper I make, he with difficulty lifting spoonful after spoonful to his mouth; then, after watching a couple of hours of TV, he goes to bed. I join him two hours later, slipping quietly between the sheets so he won't wake. He tells me he has to force his body to move from its supine position in the morning, he has to push himself mentally and physically to swing his feet—what an effort—from the mattress to the floor. The long hours of sleep don't revive him.

We try to be cheerful for each other, but I can see the strain being upbeat causes him. I worry, I feel sad for him, but I often feel the cold grip of self-pity. When I fell yesterday as I was beating the branches of the cherry tree free of snow, I wanted to stay in the icy drift, let my head sink, close my eyes, and not wake up for a hundred years. I wanted to make a snow angel that could lift me out of here, fly me high into the clouds, let me float above the troubled earth, a cold crystal being returning to its starting place, refusing to come home.

The house is closing in on us. We've never spent so many hours together—usually one of us is on the road every other month—yet I've never felt so alone. I've mentally and physically removed myself from friends, whom I rarely see. Who will take care of me if I get sick? I whine in my head. Who will shop, cook, see that I take my medication? Who will be there to say the final words I'll hear and who will know where to scatter my remains? And finally, a question I must ask: Who am I if not a companion to my beloved?

Have I narrowed myself to this parameter? Is it a bad thing for me to be so connected, so self-defined by my relationship with him? I know I'm not the only one who's made this bargain. Four centuries ago, Shakespeare wrote, in *Henry IV*: "For where thou art, there is the world itself . . . And where thou art not, desolation."

## A SMALL AMBITION

To be no more than mist
rising above the rushes,
entering the white
limbs of the trees.

For just one hour
to be a calmness,
a lifting up
minus bones and muscles,

minus memory
and cognition
and your own insistent
longing to last.

Patrick has so many skills beyond writing. He built a garden shed and three practical and exquisitely designed gates, he crafted a walnut box to hold his mother's remains, he strung for me a necklace of red beads when he was in Peru ten years ago. He can iron a shirt or blouse like a wardrobe assistant for a prince or queen. As a child he claimed he was going to be a visual artist when he grew up. He became a writer instead, I heard him say, because he couldn't afford to buy tubes of paint. In the early seventies, he found a cheaper way to bring his inner visions to life on paper: pointillist drawings with a fine-nibbed pen and black ink. Several of them appeared in his book *Unborn Things* in 1975.

Our first year together in Winnipeg I watched him painstakingly and with uncanny patience apply dot after dot after dot to big sheets of artist's paper, the images growing out of those small specks into something recognizable and fully formed. He did three portraits that year: one of Dorothy Livesay, then David Arnason, and Alden Nowlan. Alden's appeared on the cover of his last book, *The Gardens of the Wind*. After those portraits, Patrick carried around a small bouquet of pens bound with an elastic band, but with one exception I never saw him draw again. I used to bug him, ask why he was wasting such a talent. "If I could do what you do," I said, "I'd draw in between bouts of writing when the words don't come."

"Well, I'm not you, Lorna," he'd say, and I'd know to mind my own business.

One side effect of his artistic ability is his skill at drawing maps. I'd ask him to show me how to get to an office building downtown, an entrance to a somewhat hidden old-growth forest near Honeymoon Bay on Vancouver Island where we both led workshops, the exact spot where we'd scattered my father's ashes on the farm so we could find it again sixteen years later to do the same for my mother. His directions on paper, so clear and accurate, always led me to where I needed to go.

Now I want to ask him to draw a map that will show us how to get off this path we're on, how to find an open clearing where there'll be some peace for him and me, some soft natural light we can bask in. A destination where all illness will be erased. Take a left here, and at the end of the road, pull over, I want him to say to me, his handwriting and pencil strokes strong and certain. You'll find what you're looking for if you just follow this. I want it to be him, free of pain, at the end of the line he draws on the paper. I want to lie down with him, my head on his broad shoulder, my nostrils breathing in his familiar, pre-sick smell, around us the click of dragonfly wings, the low hum of bees.

We hear on the radio that this has been the biggest snowfall on Vancouver Island in a hundred years. And unlike other harsh winters, the snow is hanging around. It's deep and compressed enough by its own weight for a chunky raccoon to saunter across its hardened surface from the door of my study around the back of the yard to the tree in front of the kitchen. He climbs it easily and glances at me over his shoulder as if I don't matter. He agilely jumps to the railing where the wisteria by the end of April will pump out blossoms and fill the air with their distinctive mauve perfume. Patrick has been three months out of the hospital. He tells me no matter what he'll not go back.

We sit on the couch in the living room in the early morning and watch the shrubs and trees in the front yard and the big conifers across the road pull themselves into visibility, into the soft gaze of the dawn. Because of all the snow, out of place here, the world outside our windows is blue, the blue of my childhood, as if high above the trees a glass bottle of India ink has been tipped into the light. The darkness disappears slowly. Though I worry about what will happen next, about how many weeks we'll have before another crisis, I choose hour by hour to live with hope rather than despair, with closeness rather than distance, with the belief that if I don't risk everything, the days will be dry and shrunken, if I don't give myself over, time and time again, to love, I will not be worthy of the small space and span I've been allotted on this cherished patch of earth with my charming, brilliant, beloved husband. Forty years, one man, one woman, five cats: this adds up to a life, a palmful of time, a plenitude, a significance.

*Above me, clouds drifted east across Georgia Strait to the Coast
Mountains and the wind I could see but could not hear went its way
to the far valley I grew up in. Bright water flowed from the bamboo spout
and purled upon the sandstone before falling in the pond among
the lily pads and their oily blossoms of white and yellow and red.
A golden koi broke the pond's surface and then slid back into the shadowed
water. Basho appeared from under a budding rhododendron and Roxy stood
on a stepping stone and cleaned her white paws in the sun. My new wife
called to me and I answered her and she came down and sat beside me
in the stillness of an ordinary Sunday morning.*

Patrick Lane, *There Is a Season*

# Postscript

## March 8, 2019

I WAKE BEFORE dawn and roll over to turn on the bedside radio
as I do every morning to catch the weather and the news. Five a.m.
What comes to me in the dark is a rich baritone, *Some days there's
just too much rain*. Oh, Patrick—it's my love reading a line from one
of his poems. At first, I'm warmed by the intimacy of his voice
washing over me; a second later, when I register what's happened,
the cold crashes in. He has drifted into our bedroom from an
impossible place, yet I can't see him, can't feel his breath on my
skin, or brush the sweat from his high forehead with my fingers.

The news announcer says, "The Canadian writer Patrick Lane,
whose award-winning poetry was celebrated for its beautiful writing and its deft examination of the human condition, died last
night of a heart attack. He was seventy-nine . . ."

*No worst, there is none*—the opening of the darkest of Gerard
Manley Hopkins' dark sonnets, written over a hundred years ago.
Now the words are mine.

Patrick's head is not on the pillow beside me. When I slide my
leg over to the other side of the bed, nothing is there. I want to

burrow under the covers and never get up. Who am I if not my beloved's? How will I go on?

The mattress gives beside me, and I feel a bump against my hip. I breathe in the smell of the garden and the night clinging like dew to our cat's long hair. It's Po Chu, the one I can't pick up or snuggle, the one who makes it difficult to love. She's been out for hours. Last night when I got back from the hospital, blunted with sadness, hollowed out, I couldn't find her. Does she know that Patrick, who saved her, who taught me to be patient and kind so she could make a home with us, is gone?

I'm stunned by Patrick's absence, turning over and over the rich tones of his voice in this loneliest of hours, my first awakening into life without him.

*Some days there's just too much rain.*

The one we cherish is not coming home. Never again will he push through the gate or call my name as he steps through the door. The last of our cats, using all the might in her half-wild body, wills me to push back the covers, put my feet on the floor and walk down the hall to the kitchen.

It's just us now.

She wants her breakfast, she wants to be fed. This I can do— this one small thing I can do—a spoon, a can, a dish—with him not here. Outside the kitchen window, past the bamboo where we watched the sun reclaim the sky so many mornings, there's just a hint of light, thin enough to slip inside any kind of wound.

The poems in the book come from the
following collections by Lorna Crozier

*The House the Spirit Builds* (2019)
    "Breakage", pages 139-140
    "A Small Ambition", page 207

*What the Soul Doesn't Want* (2017)
    "Self-Centred", page 193

*The Wild in You: Voices from the Forest and the Sea* (2015)
    Lines from "Thoreau Said a Walk Changes the Walker", page 85
    "A Good Place", page 114

*The Wrong Cat* (2015)
    "Game", page 7
    "Old Style", page 42
    "Photographer", page 169
    "The Mask", pages 172-174

*Small Mechanics* (2011)

"Because We Are Made of Mostly Water", pages 58-59

"The Hour of Snow", pages 72-73

Lines from "Someone Must Be Drowning", page 100

"Finally", pages 111

"My Last Erotic Poem", pages 116-117

*The Blue Hour of the Day: Selected Poems* (2007)

"In Moonlight", page 3

Lines from "Thomas Hardy's Heart", pages 9-10

"Blizzard", page 36

"Living Day by Day", pages 55-56

"A Good Day to Start a Journal", pages 65-66

"Beauty", page 130

"A Kind of Love", pages 151-152

"Waiting for a Sign", pages 165-166

*Whetstone* (2005)

"It Is Night", page 51

"No Music In It", page 88

*What the Living Won't Let Go* (1999)

"Walking Into the Future", pages 23-24

Lines from "Golden and the River", page 121

*Everything Arrives at the Light* (1995)

"Fire Breather", pages 61-62

"A Summer's Singing", page 82

Lines from "If I Call Stones Blue", page 107

Lines from "He's Only a Cat", page 146

*Inventing the Hawk* (1992)
  "Recipes", pages 97-98

*Angels of Flesh, Angels of Silence* (1988)
  "Domestic Scene", page 104

*The Garden Going On Without Us* (1985)
  "Love Song", pages 159-160

*No Longer Two People* (1979)
  Lines on page 19

*Inside Is the Sky* (1976)
  Lines on page 27

"Inside a Needle", page 181 first published in *Riddle Fence*

Previously unpublished poems
  "Poem Me", page xi
  "The Cat We Called Basho", pages 199-200

# Acknowledgements

I started this book when Patrick fell ill because I didn't know how else to go on, to survive the days of confusion and fear. I didn't show him the parts about his hospitalization or my constant worry because I didn't want to burden him with my sadness. He had enough to carry, and our hold on the days was so tenuous. I did, however, talk to him about what I was writing, and I read him the sections about our cats and our early years together. He told me to keep going, to write the book though I know now, he was aware he'd never get to read it. I was, I *am* blessed by his writer's under-standing, in the midst of his own distress, of my need to find words for the darkest and most resplendent of things in our forty years together.

Some of the writing about my parents and my childhood, I touched on in my first memoir, *Small Beneath the Sky*. What I wrote about Carol Shields' death appeared in an earlier version in *Geist*. The section on the poet Bashō was informed by Jane Hirshfield's *Ten Windows*. The haiku that haloed his hat and that I quote on page 125 was translated "loosely," as she says, by her and Mariko Aritani. The quotations from Mary Pratt come from *The Art of*

*Mary Pratt* (Goose Lane and the Beaverbrook Art Gallery, 1995) and *Mary Pratt* (Goose Lane, 2013).

I want to thank those who have been on this journey with me, my stepsons Richard and Michael Lane and their families, my friends who wouldn't let me do this alone, especially Tina Biello, Sandra Pohan Dawkins, Seán Virgo, and Rhonda Ganz. I owe gratitude as well to Susan Musgrave, Elizabeth Philips, Don Enright and Cheryl Rowley, Mary McGovern, Suzanne and Ray Clary, Sandra Campbell, Kevin Paul, Eric McCormack, and Sharon Doobenen.

And then there is my agent, Dean Cooke, and my friends at McClelland & Stewart, Jared Bland, Ruta Liormonas, and Kelly Joseph, my sensitive, brilliant editor. The book wouldn't have seen the light of day without their belief in it. Thanks, too, to Melanie Little for her copyediting and Emma Dolan for her brilliant design.

© Angie Abdou

LORNA CROZIER is the author of seventeen books of poetry, including *God of Shadows*, *What the Soul Doesn't Want*, *The Wrong Cat*, *Small Mechanics*, *The Blue Hour of the Day: Selected Poems*, and *Whetstone*. She is also the author of *The Book of Marvels: A Compendium of Everyday Things* and the memoir *Small Beneath the Sky*, which won the Hubert Evans Award for Creative Nonfiction. She won the Governor General's Literary Award for Poetry for *Inventing the Hawk* and three additional collections were finalists for the Governor General's Literary Award for Poetry. She has received the Canadian Authors Association Award, three Pat Lowther Memorial Awards, the Raymond Souster Award, and the Dorothy Livesay Poetry Prize. She was awarded the BC Lieutenant Governor's Award for Literary Excellence and the George Woodcock Lifetime Achievement Award. She is a Professor Emerita at the University of Victoria and an Officer of the Order of Canada, and she has received five honorary doctorates for her contributions to Canadian Literature. Born in Swift Current, Saskatchewan, she now lives in British Columbia.